SKETCHES
FROM A
NORTH BEACH
JOURNAL

SKETCHES FROM A NORTH BEACH JOURNAL

*Heroes and Heroines,
the Wise and the Wily:
San Franciscans from
the Gold Rush to Yesterday*

BY ERNEST BEYL

GRIZZLY PEAK PRESS

For information contact:

Grizzly Peak Press
350 Berkeley Park Boulevard
Kensington, CA 94707
grizzlypeakpress.com

Sketches from a North Beach Journal is published by Daniel N. David
and is distributed by Grizzly Peak Press.

Front cover photos from top to bottom: The Cockettes; (second row)
Francis Ford Coppola; (third row left to right) Gold Rush Era
Prostitutes, Phyllis Diller, Jeanette Etheredge and Sean Penn; (fourth
row) Victor Hirtzler; (bottom row left to right) Herb Caen, Tony Serra

Design, layout and typesetting by
Sara B. Brownell • sarabbrownell.com

ISBN Number: 978-0-9839264-6-7
Library of Congress Number: 2015940501

Printed in the United States of America

"The miners came in forty-nine,
The whores in fifty-one;
And when they got together,
They produced the Native Son."

~ 19th Century San Francisco doggerel

"It's an odd thing but anyone who disappears
is said to be seen in San Francisco. It must be
a delightful city and possess all the attractions
of the next world."

~ Oscar Wilde, 1890

It's mad city, inhabited by perfectly insane
people whose women are of remarkable beauty.

~ Rudyard Kipling, 1891

Table of Contents

Introduction

SAN FRANCISCO is a beautiful place—a peninsula at the end of the continent, the Pacific Ocean on one side, the blue bay on the other, capped with hills, ringed by mountains. The Europeans were impressed when they first saw it at the end of the 18th century. When the first American ships sailed into San Francisco Bay the mariners remarked on the beautiful and almost empty land.

"If California ever becomes a prosperous place, this bay will be the center of its prosperity," Richard Henry Dana wrote about a voyage to San Francisco in 1836.

San Francisco had everything but people; it had beauty but no charm, no character. It was people that made San Francisco what it is. As it turned out, San Francisco is more than just a pretty face.

It takes a bit of something—something different—to be a San Franciscan. It is a different city, a western city in the sense that it is on the Pacific Coast, but this is not the West of mountains or plains. In a sense this is a city that is west of the West, as the phrase goes. It is a city on the edge of the continent—"at the end of our streets is sunset," the poet George Sterling wrote.

North of the center of the city, west of the bay, between Telegraph and Russian hills, San Francisco has a neighborhood with its own edge. This is North Beach, a place where immigrants came, from Italy and China, from Ireland and Kansas, from all over the world. Some were born in North Beach and some came there to be poets, or promoters, bartenders or baseball players, to be artists or lawyers. Many were famous and some were crazy. All are characters in this sketchbook of historic North Beach.

Ernie Beyl, who has lived in the neighborhood for many years and knows it as well as anybody, takes us through the district's past, down alleys, along streets, into famous places and forgotten ones, offering "sketches" of life in his corner of San Francisco.

North Beach to him is a city inside a city. Here are quick word portraits, like pencil sketches by a sidewalk artist, of the characters of years ago, who helped give San Francisco its early flavor. Oofty Goofty, the sideshow performer, Lola Montez, the dancer, Lotta Crabtree, Emperor Norton, all the usual suspects.

But then the sketches get more complex, more varied, bolder strokes, different folks. There are writers like Herbert Gold and Lawrence Ferlinghetti and the Beats. There is a madam or two; there are performers like Sweet Pam of the Cockettes, famous in their day, who were gay before it was fashionable. There are sketches of jazz in the clubs, a pause for an Irish Coffee with Stanton Delaplane, the newspaper guy, for a drink with Ed Moose, the incomparable host.

A quick sketch of Grimes Poznikov, who called himself the Automatic Human Jukebox, and one of Gayle Spiegelman, the Topless Mother of Eight.

This is a sketchbook of informal word portraits, not a fine arts catalogue. It chronicles a part of town that Stan Delaplane remembered fondly, where "The days were filled with sun." And at night there are characters like Don Asher, musician from Massachusetts , who discovered he could make a living as a piano player in a saloon, or Lenny Bruce, who challenged the legal criteria for obscenity.

And Ernie Beyl, who wrote this sketchbook, summed it up: "What a great city, I thought."

You might come to agree with him.

CARL NOLTE
San Francisco Chronicle reporter
and "Native Son" columnist

Foreword

SAN FRANCISCO'S NORTH BEACH neighborhood has been predominantly Italian since the early days when immigrants from the Mediterranean flocked to this section of the tiny California Gold Rush town because it reminded them of home. They became fishermen, merchants, restaurant operators, bankers, priests, poets and sports stars. And many of them made—and still make—red wine in their basements.

Today North Beach is a laid back enclave of Southern Mediterranean ambience where you are likely to hear Italian spoken more than English. But now the old Italian neighborhood is intermingled with Asians who have added their own languages, cultures and lifestyles. While Italian grandfathers are enjoying their morning lattes at sidewalk cafes or playing bocce ball a few blocks away near Joe DiMaggio Playground, energetic Chinese are practicing Tai Chi in Washington Square, one of the finest outdoor urban spaces anywhere. The result is a vibrant, cultural hodge-podge—a San Francisco treasure, an exciting place to live or, if you're a visitor, to dine, shop or just walk the streets.

San Franciscans have long had a fascination with larger than life characters—from heroes and heroines to scoundrels—who have added a sense of vigor and excitement to this city. Many of these large scale figures have lived, worked or just hung out in North Beach.

These sketches present some of the distinctive contributors to the laid back, *laisse faire* atmosphere and attitudes of the old neighborhood.

Some of the Sketches in this book have appeared in *Northside San Francisco,* the *Marina Times, North Beach Journal,* the *Nob Hill Gazette, Literary Potpourri, Saveur* or elsewhere in other formats and versions.

ERNEST BEYL

PART ONE

It All Began with the Gold

GOLD RUSH SAN FRANCISCO was rambunctious and disorderly. It was overrun by a motley crew of adventurers—both men and women—from all over the world. Along with the gold seekers, get-rich-quick ruffians and con-artists came merchants, farmers, clerks, clergy, bankers, doctors, poets, prostitutes, lawyers, sailors, salesmen, speculators and just plain seekers of the good life. Some just liked the climate and wanted to live in the European-styled city by the Golden Gate. By 1875 the population was 190,000. In 1900 it was 350,000.

Oofty Goofty and Big Bertha

Left: "Oofty Goofty" Leonard Borchardt; right: Bertha Heyman,
a.k.a. "Big Bertha the Confidence Queen"
PHOTOS: WIKIMEDIA COMMONS

SAN FRANCISCANS have always had a good sense of humor. Comedy and comic situations abounded, even in the raw-boned town's early days.

Before gold was discovered at Sutter's Mill on January 24, 1848, San Francisco was a sleepy, fog-bound village. Once news of gold got out, the sparsely populated hamlet was soon overrun with miners, merchants, farmers, clerks, entrepreneurs, sailors, ruffians, con men and prostitutes from many parts of the world. They all wanted to get rich and they all wanted entertainment. Plays, ballets, pantomimes, blackface minstrel shows and comic skits were performed in the saloons, dance halls and theaters of the "instant city" San Francisco.

Given the social values and pop culture of the time, minstrel shows with their lively tunes, fast dances and sharp witticisms, attracted large audiences. One troupe, the well-known Philadelphia Minstrels, came out from the East in 1849 and played the notorious gambling and music hall, the Bella Union on Portsmouth Square, right near today's North Beach.

In 1850 a druggist, Dr. D. J. "Doc" Robinson, who liked to do comic impersonations of prominent citizens, opened a small theater on California Street near the Customs House and called it the Dramatic Museum. It seated 280 wild and raucous entertainment seekers and featured topical satire. "Doc" Robinson's partner in the venture, James Evrard, gave occasional performances there as a female impersonator. A big hit of the time was a humorous skit titled Seeing the Elephant that ridiculed the gullibility of miners who joined the Gold Rush simply because they heard fantastic tales of picking up chunks of gold in the muddy streets.

Also in 1850, the Jenny Lind Theater opened above the Parker House saloon on Portsmouth Square. Before it burned down a few months later, several comedies by Shakespeare were drawing happy audiences.

In a Market Street sideshow in the 1860s a small thin actor was covered in horsehair and billed as the "Wild Man from Borneo." He called himself Oofty Goofty. Over at the Bella Union a self-styled wealthy widow known as Big Bertha was singing and performing skits to packed houses. The management brilliantly chose to pair Oofty Goofty with Big Bertha in a colossal performance—Shakespeare's *Romeo and Juliet*. Big Bertha, who tipped the scales at 280 pounds, was too heavy for the balcony scene. She read Juliet's lines from the floor of the stage. Oofty Goofty played Romeo from the balcony.

A Publicist for the Gold Rush

Second from left: Alta California (Book and Job Printing). Other buildings in this image include: California Restaurant, Louisiana, Sociedad, Drugs & Medicines Wholesale & Retail, Henry Johnson & Co, Bella Union, A. Holmes
PHOTOS: WIKIMEDIA COMMONS

SAN FRANCISCO newspaper history is replete with notable journalists who stride through the long public record in brittle, yellow clippings. Like some sports heroes and movie stars, journalists can be vain, self-centered, egotistical and frequently irreverent. Some like to get their names in the papers. They can also be intelligent, perceptive, witty, dedicated, good conversationalists, good storytellers, and good writers imbued with a sense of mission. And, they have their cliques and claques—followers who also like to get their names in the papers. In the history of San Francisco newspapers—that is from the 1800s to today—a few seminal figures, superstars if you will, have risen to the top like fresh cream. Sam Brannan was one of these.

On July 9, 1846 Commodore John D. Sloat, Commander-in-Chief of the U.S. Naval Forces in the Pacific, arrived at what would later be called San Francisco aboard his sloop-of-war USS Portsmouth. He raised the American flag in a dusty plaza in the tiny Mexican village called Yerba Buena. A few days later, 200 Mormons let by Sam Brannan, a printer from New York, arrived aboard a chartered vessel, the Brooklyn. The Mormons had traveled around the Horn to the Sandwich Islands, where Brannan armed his Mormon Latter Day Saints with rifles and set out for the Golden Gate.

Brannan brought with him a complete flour mill, a printing press and considerable moxie. It was his intention to start a Mormon enclave in Yerba Buena, but at about the same time, Brigham Young and his followers crossed the Rockies and discovered the Salt Lake Valley, and that was that.

But Brannan, a gambler, big spender and wheeler-dealer, was undeterred. His followers accused him of misusing funds he managed for them, and that was the end of his Mormon dream. Instead he became a newspaper publisher. However, before Brannan got around to his publishing venture, Walter Colton a former Navy chaplain who had become *alcalde*, or mayor, of the California capitol of Monterey, and Dr. Robert Semple, a dentist there, became the state's first newspapermen. On August 15, 1846 they published the *Californian*, a weekly devoted largely to shipping news. It appeared for nine months, half in Spanish, half in English.

But the discredited and resilient Sam Brannan did succeed in publishing the first newspaper in the tiny bayside village of Yerba Buena on October 24, 1846, thereby becoming the father of San Francisco journalism.

When gold was discovered at Sutter's Mill, January 24, 1848, Brannan not only published the startling news, but he shouted it in the streets and took off for the gold fields himself. That's how he became a publicist for the California Gold Rush.

The Minstrel from Stanford

BERT WILLIAMS was a native of Antigua in the West Indies. He was the first African American accepted at Stanford University. In the 1880s he became a performer with a small black minstrel troupe playing in San Francisco's Barbary Coast saloons. His salary was $7 a week.

However, a man of considerable dignity, he refused to apply the usual burnt cork mask to his face. Years later, Williams, handsome and light-skinned, achieved great success as a comic entertainer and did apply the blackface makeup.

"Come Right In, Sit Right Down, Make Yourself at Home," words by Bob White & Alfred Anderson; music by Will. H. Dixon. sheet music cover, 1909, with photograph of Vaudeville headliner and recording star Bert Williams
PHOTO: WIKIMEDIA COMMONS

He said he found the mask liberating. "… Just for a lark I blacked my face and tried the song, 'Oh I Don't Know, You're not so Warm.' Nobody was more surprised than I was when it went over like a house on fire. Then I began to find myself. It was not until I was able to see myself as another person that my sense of humor developed."

The Bordellos and the Madams

"The Ladies" of Barbary Coast, San Francisco, CA 1890
PHOTO: SAN FRANCISCO HISTORY CENTER, SAN FRANCISCO PUBLIC LIBRARY

LET'S DEAL WITH SAN FRANCISCO BORDELLOS, BAGNIOS, BROTHELS and perhaps the most appealing of these synonyms, parlor houses.

Before the California Gold Rush began in 1849 women were few and far between in the sleepy, Mexican village of Yerba Buena. There were only about 500 inhabitants, mostly men, the rare spouse and a few prostitutes from Mexico or South America. But the Gold Rush changed everything. Once those yellow tracings were found at

Sutter's Mill and word got out, almost 25,000 gold seekers arrived within six months in what had by then become San Francisco. Of this number, only about 500 were women. It's not necessary to be a skilled sociologist to find that off-balance ratio intriguing as well as instructive.

As early as the winter of 1849-50 there were already crude bordellos in San Francisco. They were found in tents and lean-tos around Portsmouth Square, along the nearby waterfront and on the slopes of Telegraph Hill. Over the next fifty or sixty years the figure grew exponentially and San Francisco gained a worldwide reputation as a wide open town.

But, if the lavish parlor houses attracted a never-ending clientele, so did the many cribs and dives of the infamous Barbary Coast where harlots plied their trade. The Barbary Coast sprang to life during the Gold Rush and operated openly until 1914 when the California Legislature passed the Red-light Abatement Act. As early as 1854 the city had enacted an anti-prostitution law but it was enforced only irregularly and with discrimination against Chinese and other minorities. These efforts toward reform didn't really slow things down. Then along came the great San Francisco Earthquake and Fire of 1906. That interrupted the lucrative trade, but not for long. Soon it was business as usual. The bordellos continued to operate right through World War II when amazingly one on Telegraph Hill was operated by a U.S. government spook agency surreptitiously conducting mind-control experiments with LSD on nocturnal visitors. The illicit but tolerated businesses continued through the 1980s—perhaps later.

Are there bordellos in the city now? The answer to that question is debatable, not easy to confirm. Gathering information on such establishments and their madams is a bit like tracking a moving target. Today, the economics of keeping up a fancy parlor house don't seem to work anymore. Property values, rental costs, all the trappings of elegant mansions decorated on a grand scale and occupied by dedicated and charming "boarders" represents an investment that seems out of synch with the times. Further, the telephone (now certainly the cell phone) has altered the course of prostitution. The call girl, the street hooker and the conscientious amateur who engages in her own individual enterprise, have eclipsed those grand social palaces of yesteryear.

The true parlor house wasn't just all about sex. Much like that other communal institution, the saloon, the parlor house was a sanctuary, a retreat from the rigors of the day. It was a friendly hideaway, a place of conviviality, where everyone knew your name, or at least did within a few minutes of your arrival. It was a private club, artfully furnished. It cosseted visitors and lavished them with attention—conversation, champagne, good food. There was frequently music for dancing; in the early days a mechanical, coin-operated machine, sometimes a pianist. For those guests who occasionally spent more than just an hour or so and languished there for the entire night, a restorative breakfast was served. Clothes were pressed. Shoes were shined. Lore has it that the girls were bright, witty and beautiful and the madams had hearts of gold just like in the movies. While the parlor houses played to a male audience, it was even whispered that there was at least one equal opportunity house where frisky establishment ladies could discreetly engage resident male companions. Early accounts of San Francisco's bawdy and wanton past confirm this.

Perhaps the colorful history of bordellos in San Francisco is best told through portraits of a few of the many madams who brought them to life. Students of this off-color aspect of the city would do well to remember that the difference between a madam and a prostitute may be marginal. Undoubtedly one can lead to the other—or vice versa. Nevertheless, San Francisco's madams have always been a bit like her celebrity chefs—colorful and single-minded.

San Francisco's First Madam

IRENE McCREADY is generally credited with being the first madam in San Francisco. She came to the fast-growing town in April of 1849 with her rakish lover, James McCabe who opened a gambling hall called El Dorado in a tent on Portsmouth Square. It soon became a magnet for the free-spirited miners with gold dust in their jeans. Irene, with McCabe's backing, opened a simple bagnio nearby in a one-story, frame building. It burned down, as did El Dorado, within a few months in San Francisco's first-of-a-series of disastrous fires. El Dorado opened again and so did Madam McCready's establishment. A few months later the McCready bagnio burned to the ground again. She acquired a two-story brick building and she was back in business with a plush and proper parlor house. She operated it through 1856. It was reported that her clientele included a California governor, a senator and a number of judges. She and McCabe had a stormy and memorable relationship. Believing he was cheating on her, she drugged him and when he passed out, she shaved him head to toe which effectively put him out of action for some time. McCabe eventually gave up gambling and took up the law, practicing in San Francisco. Unfortunately, history has lost track of Irene McCready.

———

A Chinese Beauty Named Ah Toy

A 20-YEAR-OLD CHINESE PROSTITUTE, Ah Toy, arrived in San Francisco about 1848 and soon was set up in a small shanty in what was destined to become San Francisco's Chinatown. Years later she said she came to San Francisco to "better her condition." And better it she did. Ah Toy was a tall woman with an aristocratic bearing and quite beautiful. Soon she began keeping company with a vigilante police officer named John A. Clark. In 1850 she made the jump to madam and gave employment to five young Chinese women. Her parlor house was located in an alley called Pike Street. Today it is Waverly Place in Chinatown.

Not at all shy, Ah Toy used the judicial system to her advantage and appeared in court several times when she felt she was wronged. Once she brought a complaint against miners who she said had cheated her by paying her fees in brass filings instead of gold. The charges were eventually dismissed. Later she was arrested and convicted for keeping a disorderly house, highly unusual since Caucasian madams and their "boarders" were seldom bothered by the law. This happened several times and she finally left the business, married and later sold clams in the South Bay town, Alviso. She lived to within a few days of her one hundredth birthday.

Belle Cora and the Vigilantes

BELLE CORA, a leading San Francisco madam of the 1850s, claimed to be the daughter of a Baltimore minister. She said that at 17 she had been seduced and left pregnant. Her father cast her out penniless and she wound up in New Orleans. She said the baby died in childbirth and having no options she became a prostitute in a local parlor house. There she came to the attention of a prominent gambler, Charles Cora, who took her under his wing.

Another version of the Belle Cora story goes like this: In her early teens she became a dressmaker and worked on fancy garments for prostitutes in a Baltimore parlor house. Tired of sewing, she joined the ranks of the parlor house girls and later moved to Charleston. She either met Cora there or in New Orleans. Sensing opportunity, Belle and Cora sailed for San Francisco, arriving late in 1849. Cora gambled from one mining town to another and Belle, a striking brunette later described by a San Francisco detective as a "voluptuous creature," tagged along. In the early 1850s she opened a simple bordello in the California mining town of Sonora. Later, Charles Cora and Belle, now calling herself Belle Cora, moved to San Francisco and she opened a parlor house on Dupont Street, now Grant Avenue. It was said to be nondescript on the outside and lavishly appointed inside. Then, in 1855, she moved to a two-story brick building nearby.

A Methodist minister, the Reverend William Taylor, who tirelessly shamed the fallen sisterhood, described Belle Cora's parlor house like this: "...magnificent without, beautiful within, furnished with Brussels velvet, silk and damask. Heavy furniture of rosewood, and walls hung with beautiful paintings, and music from a pianoforte, melodeon, and harp; no house more prominent or beautiful for situation in the city."

In 1855 Charles Cora shot and killed a U.S. Marshall over a presumed snub of social-climbing Belle. In spite of her struggles to save Cora, he was hanged in May of 1856 by the Vigilance Committee operating in San Francisco at the time. The day of the hanging Belle married Charles Cora. There were suggestions that Belle be banished from San Francisco, but she also had her defenders. She mourned for a while then it was business as usual. She was 29 when Cora was hung. She died at 35 in 1862.

In 1916 Pauline Jacobson published a serial on Belle Cora in the *San Francisco Bulletin*. As a result the madam was disinterred from Calvary Cemetery and laid to rest with her gambler husband beneath a common headstone at Mission Dolores.

Madame Mustache

Eleanor Dumont a.k.a. Madam Mustache, the image is in dispute
PHOTO: COURTESY LEGENDSOFAMERICA.COM

PERHAPS NOT in the same league with such superstars as Irene McCready, Ah Toy and Belle Cora, but nevertheless an interesting footnote to the San Francisco parlor house saga, was a French woman, Eleanor Dumont. She was known—behind her back, one hopes—as Madam Mustache, for her distinguishing feature described by one chronicler as growing with "Mediterranean luxuriousness." From 1854 Madam Mustache gambled and "madamed" her way around California's gold towns. She also wandered as far as Idaho, Montana and Wyoming. At one point Madam Mustache had 15-year-old Jane Canary—Calamity Jane, she was called—as one of her "boarders." Apparently Calamity Jane not only worked in brothels but patronized them as well, believing that in male drag she could fool any prostitute. She also took pride in the fact that she was once thrown out of a Bozeman, Montana whorehouse for being a bad influence. Eventually, tiring of traveling what later became known as the parlor house circuit, Madam Moustache opened her own place in San Francisco sometime between the late 1860s and mid-1870s. It didn't last very long and we are told that she committed suicide in 1879.

----·•·----

"Diamond Jessie" Hayman

A MADAM WHO STANDS OUT during the period just before and after the San Francisco Earthquake and Fire of 1906 was "Diamond Jessie" Hayman. She was fond of calling her parlor house on Ellis Street "an oasis from cares and time." The story of New Orleans-born "Diamond Jessie" spanned a period from the 1890s and up to the time of Prohibition (1920). At the time she called herself Jessie Mellon and was a "boarder" at the Ellis Street house of a madam named Nina Hayman. Later, after the tall, slender and raven-tressed Jessie had a series of trysts with a Russian Grand Duke who was on a world tour, she took over the madam's name, the business and became wealthy, always believing that diamonds were a girl's best friend.

Arnold Genthe, the San Francisco photographer, who seems to have arranged the liaison between the royal Russian and the engaging prostitute, described her by saying "She had the face and figure of an empress, and the pose and manner of one as well." Jessie operated, what amounted to a chain of parlor houses. It wasn't until 1917 that she was forced to close them down by a combination of social reform legislation and a crusade against vice by religious interests. She retired gracefully to a house—in this case, let's call it a home—on Jackson Street. She died in a London hotel while on a tour of the world.

"I Shot Him Because I Loved Him"

A NATIVE SAN FRANCISCAN born in the Mission District in 1869, blonde and flamboyant Tessie Wall became a madam in the city's Tenderloin early in the 1900s. She apparently had a tremendous capacity for champagne and once is reported to have outlasted world champion boxer John L. Sullivan in a drinking bout while she worked as a dancehall girl in a Market street dive. Her parlor house, first on Larkin Street, then on O'Farrell Street, was popular with a young college-boy clientele. She later married gambler Frank Daroux. After a few years of marriage, Daroux and Tessie Wall were divorced but she continued to carry the torch. When he refused to return to her she shot him but he survived. When arrested she cried out "I shot him because I love him, God damn him!" Tessie retired with a fortune and died in 1932.

Emperor Norton

Emperor Norton
PHOTO: WIKIMEDIA COMMONS

JOSHUA NORTON, son of a Jewish merchant in London, came to San Francisco in 1849 but he didn't become a miner in search of gold. He sought wealth another way. He became a businessman—a wholesale grocer. "I shall stay here till I have seen this village grow to be one of the world's greatest and most beautiful cities," he said. While newcomers hardly had time to consider the small town by the bay before striking out for the gold country, Joshua Norton stuck around. "I'll stay here and find my fortune here, and someday the men will come back from the hills, multiplied a thousand times," And he was right.

He did well. He purchased land and built stores and warehouses for his goods. He became a prominent and shrewd citizen. Other merchants sought his counsel. Today we would call him a business tycoon. He had the Midas touch. Everything he put his mind to turned to gold. In 1853 Norton attempted to corner the world's rice market. He was thinking big. He advised friends to join him in the effort and many did. And then the bubble burst.

In good faith, Norton attempted to compensate those who had lost fortunes with him. Soon he was penniless. Suddenly he was gone. He disappeared for several months in 1854. No one knew where he went.

Then, like the plot of a made-for-TV movie, he reappeared later that year. But he was a different man. At least he looked like a different man. Instead of wearing his tailored business suit and a bowler, he walked imperiously down Montgomery Street, ramrod straight, wearing a strange uniform—a uniform like none seen before. He was in military regalia complete with epaulets and campaign medals. With it he wore a high beaver hat decorated with colored feathers, and he carried a grapevine cane that looked very official.

To the astonished citizens of San Francisco he proclaimed himself Norton, the First, Emperor of the United States and Protector of Mexico. And he was serious. He had gone mad. But nicely mad. He issued his own currency and he used it to pay his expenses. And, strangely, his phony money was honored. He used it for all his needs and for the needs of his two mongrel dogs, Bummer and Lazarus, his constant companions.

The Central Pacific Railroad gave him a free pass for all its trains. He ate free of charge in the dining cars. Hedging on the hereafter, each Sunday he attended two church services—one at the Synagogue Emanu-El and one at Old St. Mary's for a Catholic mass.

Norton the First, Emperor of the United States and Protector of Mexico gave himself over to what he saw as the improvement of society. He issued proclamations and made public statements. No feminist, he opposed woman suffrage and urged woman to stay home, clean their houses and bear children. He urged friendship between the United States and England and recommended that President Abraham Lincoln marry Queen Victoria. Lincoln replied to Emperor Norton by saying he would give it consideration. Queen Victoria did not reply. Among the Emperor's ideas was this one: He suggested that a bridge be built between San Francisco and Oakland. He wasn't that mad.

Then, in 1880 at sixty-one years of age, in front of Old St. Mary's Church, he collapsed and died. Flags flew at half-staff and more than 30,000 San Franciscans attended his funeral.

———•◦•———

PART TWO

The Instant City

RIGHT FROM ITS EARLY DAYS the raw-boned, fog-bound town called San Francisco had a high degree of sophistication that belied its edge-of-the-continent isolation. The Gold Rush in 1949, the discovery of Nevada's Comstock Lode of Silver in 1857, and the completion of the transcontinental railroad in 1869, had turned this tiny village into an instant city. Suddenly San Francisco became a western metropolis with worldly tastes and enthusiasms.

"Not Even Jackassable"

ONE RECENT SUN-SPACKLED DAY in San Francisco a casually-dressed young man was standing purposively at the corner of Columbus Avenue and Broadway selling poems. For only a dollar he would recite one of his own then give a copy to the purchaser. How intelligent. How sensible. How—in that overworked phrase—"very San Francisco." Living in a city where one can buy a poem on a street corner, is almost, but not quite, as good as creating one.

To undertake a poetic history of San Francisco, in prose no less, is fraught with pitfalls—who to include, who to omit.

One of the earliest San Francisco poems was written by a comedic gold miner in 1849 who, after slipping in the deep mud at the corner of Clay and Kearny Streets, scrawled this poetic traffic warning:

> *This street is impassable*
> *Not even jackassable*

Through the years there have been many poets in San Francisco—pranksters, rhymesters, sonneteers, balladeers, rhapsodists, discontents, malcontents, misfits, storytellers, zealots, wake-up-call tacticians, shock and awe messengers, social climbers and pompous asses. At times it has been difficult to tell one from the other.

Early San Francisco spawned poets at the drop of a rhyming couplet. A devil-may-care, bohemian lifestyle made it almost mandatory that young men and women of artistic temperament give it a try. Bret Harte, Samuel Clemens, Ina Coolbrith, Jack London, Ambrose Bierce, George Sterling, Robert Louis Stevenson, Charles Warren Stoddard, Mary Austin, Joaquin Miller and many others, wrote poetry. Some of it quite good. Some mediocre. Some dreadful. The point is they wrote it. The muse was upon them.

Lola Montez and the Spider Dance

Lola Montez, 1851
PHOTO: WIKIMEDIA COMMONS

ONE OF THE BIGGEST SENSATIONS in early San Francisco was Lola Montez who brought her famous Spider Dance to San Francisco in 1853 for the gold miners. She appeared at the Bella Union on Portsmouth Square. The Bella Union began as a gambling hall in 1849 but had a small stage and soon became what was then called a melodeon—a place to watch performances, the forerunners of the burlesque show as we think of it today.

A playbill of the time stated: "Full-grown People Are Invited to Visit the Bella Union if you Want to make a Night of it. The Show is

Not of the Kindergarten Class, but Just Your Size, if You are Inclined to be Frisky and Sporty."

Lola Montez and her Spider Dance created a sensation. Patrons were hanging from the rafters the better to see Lola swat at the imaginary spiders crawling around beneath her flesh-colored tights.

Lola had arrived in San Francisco by streamer. It was said that a celebratory carriage was dragged through the streets to the Bella Union where admirers lifted her into their arms and carried her into the melodeon and deposited her on stage. After she danced her Spider Dance, we are told the audience threw bags of gold dust at her feet.

So what's the story behind the story here?

Lola Montez—Maria Eliza Dolores Rosanna Gilbert—was born in Ireland in 1818. As a youngster she traveled to India, Scotland and France with her father who was in the military. Later in Spain she learned Spanish dancing. Somewhere along the line she learned the Spider Dance and performed it at the drop of a hat, or of hard currency. As I said, she was a sensation. She died penniless in New York.

Little Lotta Crabtree

Lotta Crabtree
PHOTO: WIKIMEDIA COMMONS

LITTLE LOTTA CRABTREE was the Shirley Temple of her time—an elfin, moppet who laughed, danced and sang the tunes of the day. In 1853 Lotta and her mother came to San Francisco by steamship around the Horn from the East Coast. They were searching for John Crabtree, Lotta's father, who had taken off for the Gold Country to try his hand at mining. Lotta was six. Her mother Mary Ann, found her small daughter to be vivacious and irrepressible. And soon the child was entertaining the citizens of the rambunctious town from makeshift stages. She was a natural.

Then word came that John Crabtree was in Grass Valley in the Sierra foothills and mother and daughter joined him. There a fortuitous thing happened. Little Lotta met Lola Montez who had become an international star with her famed Spider Dance. Lola was a sensation in Grass Valley where the pickings for entertainment were slim. Lola took the winsome minx, now eight, under her charming wing.

And, as frequently happens, suddenly Little Lotta became a vivacious and beautiful young woman. She became an international star and not only performed in San Francisco but in New York, Philadelphia, Boston and London. She never married. The theater was her life.

When Lotta Crabtree died in 1924 she left an estate of nearly four million dollars. Much of that fortune she left to stray dogs and old horses.

Bohemian George Sterling

Portrait of George Sterling (1926) shortly
before his death
PHOTO: WIKIMEDIA COMMONS

THE POET WHO SEEMED to capture a young San Francisco best was George Sterling (1869-1926). Struggling to be the most bohemian in a city of struggling, would-be bohemians, Sterling, a former seminarian born on Long Island, came to Northern California only to become a real estate salesman. He wrote poetry while riding the ferryboat from the East Bay on his way to San Francisco to pursue commerce. Ambrose Bierce (1842-1914), a journalist and occasional poet himself, befriended Sterling, as did a young Jack London just out of Oakland High School. And by the way, there should be a question mark following Bierce's born-and-died statistics. He went to Mexico to join Pancho Villa's revolutionary army in 1914 but disappeared. It is assumed by many that he was shot by a revolutionary firing squad that year. Bierce's body was never located.

A surviving snippet of Bierce's poetry reads:

> *When mountains were stained as with wine*
> *By the dawning of Time, and as wine*
> *Were the seas.*

Sterling and his friends wandered bohemian San Francisco looking for wine, women and song. They found all three without difficulty. Sterling is seldom read these days but is remembered for a few lines in his work *The City by the Sea—San Francisco*.

> *At the end of our streets is sunrise;*
> *At the end of our streets are spars;*
> *At the end of our streets is sunset;*
> *At the end of our streets the stars.*

Confused and alcoholic, or vice versa, Sterling sadly took his own life by poison in his room in San Francisco's Bohemian Club.

———•———

Dr. Sun Yat-sen and Foot Binding

Left: Sun Yat-sen, circa 1912; Right: Chinese leader Sun Yat-sen, by the sculptor, Beniamino Bufano
PHOTO: WIKIMEDIA COMMONS

THERE'S A STATUE in St. Mary's Square at the corner of California Street and Grant Avenue of Dr. Sun Yat-sen, first president of the Chinese Republic which was founded in 1911. The 12-foot statue, stainless steel and red granite, was created in 1937 by Beniamino Bufano, famed Italian-American sculptor who lived in North Beach. Bufano had met the Chinese revolutionary hero while traveling in China. They became friends. Sun Yat-sen came to San Francisco in 1904 and with false documentation was admitted in spite of the odious Chinese Exclusion Act established in 1882 and not repealed until 1943. While Sun was here he was already planning to overthrow China's Ching Dynasty and set up China as a republic based somewhat on the U.S. model.

During Sun's political exile here he hid out in Chinatown on Spofford Alley and raised funds in support of his cause. When Sun's Chinese republic was founded, not the least of his reforms was the elimination of the practice of foot binding to prohibit the growth of the feet of young women.

———

Adah Isaacs Menken and Mazeppa

Adah Isaacs Menken (1835-1868), dated 1866
PHOTO: WIKIMEDIA COMMONS

CONSIDER AMERICAN ACTRESS and poet Adah Isaacs Menken. Wildly popular in wildly literary early San Francisco, Adah took the free-swinging, art-seeking city by storm as *Mazeppa*, the Lord Byron stem-winder. In her version, a tartar youth (played by Adah) is stripped by captors. As a climax she rides off stage on horseback wearing only flesh colored tights, her long black hair streaming and concealing. On opening night at Macguire's Opera House on Washington Street between Kearny and Montgomery, she charmed Bret Harte, Joaquin Miller and Charles Warren Stoddard, San Francisco's first known gay poet. San Francisco loved Adah and she, in turn loved San Francisco, or at least various prominent San Franciscans. Later she took *Mazeppa* to Paris and London.

Her best recalled poem, flamboyant and autobiographical, is Infelicia which she dedicated to her good friend Charles Dickens. A lengthy and turgid work, it ends like this:

> *Where is the promise of my years*
> *Once written on my brow?*
> *Ere errors agonies and fears*
> *Brought with them all that speaks in tears*
> *Ere I had sunk beneath my peers*
> *Where sleeps that promise now?*

She died in London in poverty and forgotten by her early admirers.

The Saga of Black Bart PO 8

NOT AS RHAPSODIC as many other San Francisco poets of the time, but a poet nevertheless, was Charles Boles, a dapper easterner who began holding up Wells Fargo stages in Northern California in the 1870s. A short man, Boles placed a derby hat on his head to give him a certain ranginess, covered himself with a large flour sack with eye holes cut out, and stood in the middle of the roadway with a shotgun. When the stagecoach stopped, Boles called out "Throw down the box," in a deep, theatrical voice. After the stagecoach had driven away in haste, Boles rifled the box and left behind one of his poems. Here's an example:

Charles Boles, aka "Black Bart"
PHOTO: WIKIMEDIA COMMONS

> *So here I've stood while wind and rain*
> *Have set the trees a sobbin'*
> *And risked my life for that damned box*
> *That wasn't worth the robbin'*

He signed his poems Black Bart, PO 8.

Black Bart was finally apprehended and sent to San Quentin but, a model prisoner, he was released in four-and-a-half years and disappeared.

Eadweard Muybridge and his Zoopraziscope

Eadweard Muybridge's Zoopraziscope: Mule Bucking and Kicking; 1893; Eadweard Muybridge
PHOTOS: WIKIMEDIA COMMONS

SAN FRANCISCO narrowly missed out on becoming the film capital of the world. Perhaps it's just as well. The city has enough narcissism and other "isms" without being "Hollywood by the Bay." Nevertheless, San Francisco, in fact most of the Northern California Bay Area, has had a long love affair with the movies.

Motion pictures were invented in 1878 down on the Leland Stanford farm in Palo Alto. The first public motion picture exhibition took place 1880 in San Francisco. The first complete movie studio on the Pacific Coast, 1906, was not in Southern California. It was in San Francisco. The classic Western with the strong, silent cowboy hero was first developed in 1907 across San Francisco Bay in Niles Canyon. Movies in color were developed across the Golden Gate in Marin County in 1918. The first "talkie," The Jazz Singer, was filmed near Union Square in 1927.

All true. None of these "firsts" happened in Southern California. So, in moviemaking parlance, let's cut to the chase.

In the 1870s railroad baron and former California Governor Leland Stanford made an intriguing wager with a friend that ultimately led to what we know today as movies. Stanford bet $25,000 that at full gallop all four of a horse's hooves are off the ground at the same time. All he had to do was prove it. In 1878 on Stanford's Palo Alto estate, an English-born photographer Eadweard Muybridge rigged a series of 24 cameras and set them to release their shutters in sequence when one of Stanford's thoroughbreds, Sallie Gardner, galloped by. The experiment proved two things. First, Stanford was correct in his assumption about galloping horses. But it was the second discovery that led to what we know today as Hollywood. Motion could be reproduced in a realistic fashion.

Then Muybridge, with financial aid from an enthusiastic Stanford, constructed a primitive, sequential photo projector called the Zoopraziscope. On May 4, 1880 Muybridge presented the first public movie screening. It was held at the San Francisco Art Association Exhibition Hall, on Pine Street between Montgomery and Kearny and was called *Illustrated Photographs in Motion*. Admission was fifty cents. The show featured the thoroughbred Sallie Gardner and a gymnast named William Lawton. Sally was the precursor to Lassie, Lawton to Arnold Schwarzenegger.

———

Alice B. Toklas and the Joy of Excess

WHEN I STARTED A SERIES OF PROFILES for *Northside San Francisco* on what I termed "Unlikely Heroes in the Gastronomic Trenches" I searched for an unlikely heroine.

I didn't want to present myself as an unconscious, male-obsessed jerk. So I did come up with some likely candidates—Eliza Acton who wrote *Modern Cookery for Private Families* in 1845, Isabella Beeton and her book *Household Management* published in 1861, and, of course, Fannie Farmer, Betty Crocker, M.F.K. Fisher and, yes indeed, Julia Child. Maybe I can come up with some Fisher stuff for another time and right now I'm all Julia Child-ed out.

But suddenly I remembered a woman I met back in the fifties— Poppy Cannon, wife of Ralph Bunche, Nobel Peace Prize-winning civil rights activist. Poppy was food editor for *House Beautiful* when I met her and she gave me a copy of a book she had just edited, *Aromas and Flavors of Past and Present* by Alice B. Toklas.

Of course—Alice B. Toklas, the Brownie Lady—as I had come to think of her. Surely she's "An Unlikely Heroine in the Gastronomic Trenches," I told myself.

Well, she is certainly that, but not for the reason that may come to readers' fertile minds (think Maryjane Brownies).

Alice was a hometown girl. She was born in San Francisco in 1877 on O'Farrell Street a block away from what is now called Alice B. Toklas Place, an alley between Polk and Van Ness.

And lest we forget, she went on to become Gertrude Stein's buddy, lover, secretary, gofer and cook. Remember it was Stein, born in Oakland, who said when she returned to visit her hometown, "There is no there, there." But living with Stein in Paris Alice experienced a lot of there, there. In Stein's Left Bank apartment on *Rue de Fleurus* young Alice met and became friendly with Henri Matisse, Pablo Picasso, Juan Gris, Georges Braque, Ernest Hemingway, Paul Bowles, Sherwood Anderson, and other creative types of the time. They came to the art-filled salon to have high discourse with Stein and to chat up Alice and eat her watercress sandwiches and her *Trout au Bleu.*

Today, at least here in San Francisco where we pay attention to such things, Alice B. Toklas is usually thought of as a pothead for a recipe that caused a sensation–"Haschich Fudge"–in her *Alice B. Toklas Cook Book,* published in 1954. "Haschich Fudge" may be seen as a forerunner to "Hippie Brownies." Here's a quote from her cookbook that will set the stage: "In the menu there should be a climax and a culmination. Come to it gently. One will suffice." Okay.

Yes, Alice was a sensualist but she really had very little to do with that mind-blowing fudge recipe. She got it from surrealist painter Brion Gysin and included it in the book at the last minute. It was kicked out of the American edition but included in the English one. Perhaps Brits were more broad-minded.

While "Haschich Fudge" might have been enough for me to name Alice an "Unlikely Heroine in the Gastronomic Trenches," I'm going the extra mile here with her for other reasons.

Alice B. (for Babette) Toklas was an epicure, and an outlandish, decadent one at that. But she didn't just talk and write sensuously about exotic cuisine, she could prepare it as well. She was an intellectual cook who believed in the gastronomic joys of excess. She was a fervent believer in the Oscar Wilde mandate "Everything in moderation, including moderation." Where is Alice now that we need her? She died in 1967.

Consider these dishes from Alice B. Toklas. Some of the titles alone should get the gastronomic juices running.

Tarte Chambord (with raspberry jam and lots of raspberry liqueur), Scheherazade's Melon (a hollow melon filled with pineapple, peaches, bananas, raspberries, wild strawberries, champagne, crème de menthe, kirsch and butter of course), Bavarian Cream Perfect Love (lots of whipped cream), Scrambled Eggs Picabia (named for the Dada painter and calls for equal parts butter and egg), Pike in Half Mourning (covered in green mayonnaise), Nymph Aurora (shrimp in heavy cream), Extravagant Mashed Potatoes (equal parts potatoes and butter) and, Short Ribs of Beef (add a beef knuckle and a calf's foot naturally).

Here's one more that deserves special comment: Bass Picasso.

This fine bass is poached in wine and butter, covered with yellow mayonnaise, then decorated with red mayonnaise, and topped with sieved hard-boiled eggs, truffles and finely chopped herbs. By the way, the red mayonnaise is not colored with catsup but with tomato paste. When Picasso was served this humble bass he is said to have suggested that Alice offer it to impressionist painter Henri Matisse.

Just like Stein and Toklas, Picasso and Matisse believed in the joy of excess.

———•———

Celebrity Chef Victor Hirtzler

Chef Victor Hirtzler
PHOTO: FROM THE COLLECTION OF HOTEL ST.
FRANCIS, SAN FRANCISCO

Joseph Beyl
PHOTO: AUTHOR'S COLLECTION

MY FATHER, JOSEPH BEYL, came to the United States from Alsace in 1912 on the steamer *Noordam*. His father, Anton Beyl, was a baker in the storybook village of Obernai, not far from Strasbourg. As a boy, my father worked in the family bakery on the ground floor of their four-story, half-timbered house. On Sundays on their way to church, Obernai *hausfrauen* dropped off *baeckeofe* (baker's oven)—sliced potatoes and onions, with whatever meat was available, and liberally dosed with an Alsatian white wine—at the bakery. It was my father's job to slide these casseroles into the huge, wood-burning oven that during the morning hours still held a high heat. Following Mass, the *hausfrauen* picked up their *baeckeofe*, bubbling and steaming, and carried them home for Sunday dinner.

When he was a youngster my father experienced the inevitable itch we all know as wanderlust. At fifteen he talked his father into allowing him to immigrate to America. So, he secured letters from his schoolmaster and from the parish priest attesting to his good character, studiousness and how he served the Catholic Church faithfully as an altar boy. A few months later he sailed from Marseilles with a small group of like-minded Alsatians bound for America.

Tangled and mangled by history, sometimes French and sometimes German, Alsace was part of the German *Vaterland* during my father's boyhood. He spoke both French and German at that time and later spoke English fluently as well.

When the ship arrived at New York my father's sponsor was inexplicably not there to meet him. Another Alsatian on the ship had already been claimed. Joseph, near tears, persuaded his shipboard friend to introduce him to her sponsor who agreed to take him as well. After the paperwork and medical examinations, they were off to Manhattan's Lower East Side to a boardinghouse run by Alsatians. A few days later my father had a job in Manhattan's Hotel Astor as a baker's assistant. Need I say that the Hotel Astor's pastry chef was Alsatian? Within a year, Joseph went to Philadelphia, where the *chef de cuisine* at the Bellevue Stratford Hotel, yet another Alsatian, signed him on as a *chef commis*.

In 1916, when he was nineteen, he moved west to San Francisco. On arrival at the end of the rail line at Oakland's train station, Joseph Beyl took a ferryboat across San Francisco Bay and disembarked at the Ferry Building. From there he made his way on foot up Market Street, turned right on Powell where the cable cars still run, and walked into the tradesman's entrance of the St. Francis Hotel. He presented himself to Chef Victor Hirtzler, who became my father's mentor.

If there had been such a thing as a celebrity chef in 1916, Victor Hirtzler would have embodied the concept. Yet another Alsatian, Hirtzler was born in Strasbourg. He was adventurous and flamboyant, terms I always liked to ascribe to my father. The year of Hirtzler's birth is unknown but in various biographies we find that he began cooking at thirteen. We are also told that Hirtzler left Strasbourg and traveled throughout Europe where he said he began cooking for European royal families. The program notes for a banquet served at San Francisco's St. Francis Hotel, dated May 25, 1982, which commemorated *chef de cuisine* Victor Hirtzler, stated "Most everyone knows that Victor was the food taster for Russia's Czar Nicholas II…"

Elsewhere, it is said that he became chef for King Don Carlos of Portugal and created elaborate dining experiences for the King and his court. One was listed as *La Mousse Faison Lucullus.* Breast of pheasant stuffed with truffles and woodcock with a sauce of Champagne and Madeira. Again, delving into the Hirtzler PR haze, it was said this dish cost $180 per serving and that in 1910 Portuguese patriots became so incensed at this extravagance that they tossed a bomb into the King's automobile and concluded that monarchy with an assassination. At that point Hirtzler decided to immigrate to the United States.

In 1916, the same year my father turned up at the St. Francis looking for work, Hirtzler, now a top chef, prepared a luncheon for United States presidential candidate, Charles Evan Hughes. The race between Hughes and Woodrow Wilson was close. California's vote was expected to be crucial. When Hughes was seated the waiters walked out on strike to make the point that they wished to be unionized. We are told that Hughes was about to honor the strike by leaving when our man Hirtzler convinced him to stay and served Hughes himself. The following day handbills circulated by the waiters claimed that Hughes was anti-union. On Election Day, Wilson defeated Hughes by—and this is too good not to quote—"10,000 votes, the exact number of workers in the union." This is according to a press release issued by the St. Francis Hotel.

Yes, Victor Hirtzler was a superstar chef before there were superstar chefs. He left the St. Francis in 1925 and returned to Strasbourg. He died in 1931. The St. Francis always took great pride in its celebrity chef and for a while, up on the hotel's 32nd floor, it operated a restaurant called Victor's.

Perhaps Hirtzler's most famous recipe was for what he called Celery Victor. Here is the recipe right out of Victor Hirtzler's cookbook. *"Wash six stalks of large celery. Make a stock with one soup hen or chicken bones, and five pounds of veal bones, in the usual manner, with carrots, onions, bay leaves, parsley, salt and whole pepper. Place celery in vessel and strain broth over same, and boil until soft. Allow to cool in the broth. When cold press the broth out of the celery gently with the hands, and place on a plate. Season with salt, fresh ground black pepper, chervil, and one-quarter white wine tarragon vinegar to three-quarters of olive oil."*

So Joseph Beyl, from a small town near Strasbourg, fell under Hirtzler's spell. When my father died in 1989 at 93, I inherited a few remnants from his long life. He left me his kitchen knives, which I use daily, and his cookbooks. Prized in that collection, is a well-thumbed first edition of the *Hotel St. Francis Cook Book,* by Victor Hirtzler, copyright 1919. In the front of the book is a photograph of Hirtzler with a copy of his bold signature just below it. He is standing in his chef's "whites" at a three-quarter angle to the camera. His arms are folded across his chest. His right shoulder is pushed forward assertively. He is a handsome man. His eyes stare strongly, right at the camera. Dark eyebrows and full, dark mustache. And a wonderful goatee. He wears his signature red fez. This photograph of Hirtzler reminds me of early photos of my father. I have one of him on a hiking expedition in Marin County, across the Golden Gate from San Francisco. He stands in hiking gear, including lace-up boots, in front of a gnarled oak. There he is at a three-quarter angle to the camera, one leg pushed forward assertively, hands clasped into fists which are punched into his hips. His elbows jut out on either side. He stares at the camera. Now that I think of it, in most photos I have of my father in his chef's "whites," he is in this same pose: leg forward, shoulder forward (rather aggressively I think now). Arms are either folded across his chest or akimbo with hands on hips. A slim man in his youth, my father later took on the shape of most chefs of the time: heavy, slightly stooped, with a legs-apart, flat-footed stance.

Hirtzler apparently liked this young fellow Alsatian. He found him a hard worker and a good student in the kitchen. So he pushed my father ahead, first as a *chef commis* and later as *sous chef* under the master. And, when Hirtzler heard about a position as *chef de cuisine* at the Hotel Californian in Fresno, he made my father apply. With Hirtzler's strong recommendation my father got the job. I have some Hotel Californian menus from 1928 and 1929. One menu in the Table D'Hote Dinner section ($1.50 for eight courses, by the way) shows Filet of Lean Cod, Belle Meuniere; Roast Saddle of Lamb with Mint Jelly and Roast Duckling with Banana Fritters. The a la carte section of the menu shows seventeen vegetables, thirteen omelets, twelve potatoes and seventeen salads, including Hirtzler's well-known Celery Victor, plain or with Crab or Lobster.

In those days there was a strong German immigrant community in Fresno and my father was a nice German (Alsatian) young man with a good job. He met my mother (a nice German girl) in a social club. Her family approved. They were married. And that's how I happened to be born in Fresno, California. Then, opportunity (read Victor Hirtzler) knocked once more. My father bought a Willy's Knight Phaeton, packed up my mother and me and drove back to San Francisco where he had a job waiting at the Alexander Hamilton Hotel as *chef de cuisine*.

Many years later, after my father had retired from almost a lifetime as a *chef de cuisine*, I asked him about Hirtzler and the influence the master had on the youngster from Alsace. He told me, "When Victor hired me at the St. Francis I was just a helper in the kitchen, but after a while he taught me everything. How to make stocks and sauces like Hollandaise and Bernaise. He taught me how to prepare and serve the various cold buffet items like salads and sandwiches. He taught me fancy desserts."

My father worked most of his professional life as a chef in hotels and restaurants in and around San Francisco. He was fond of saying that things came easy for him. Thanks to Victor Hirtzler.

Citizen Hearst's Birthday Present

William Randolph Hearst, American newspaper publisher, 1904
PHOTO: WIKIMEDIA COMMONS

THESE DAYS MOST NEWSPAPERS in San Francisco are tame lap dogs whose bark is worse than their bite. But it wasn't always that way. In times past they had a loud bark and a real bite.

In the entire history of San Francisco newspapers—that is from the mid-1800s to today—a few seminal figures, superstars if you will, have risen to the top like fresh cream in a milk bottle, if you can remember milk bottles.

Here is the cast of characters that make my personal cut. (And just for perspective, by 1775 there were 37 newspapers in America. And by 1816 there were seven daily papers in New York City alone.)

In 1846 Mormon Elder Samuel Brannan was the editor of the *California Star,* San Francisco's first newspaper, and a pitchman for California's Gold Rush. He was a hot-headed PR guy.

In the 1850s Samuel Langhorne Clemens, later to become better known as Mark Twain, was an itinerant journalist. He became a reporter for the old *San Francisco Call* and occasionally wrote for the *San Francisco Chronicle* in exchange for desk space.

Francis Bret Harte, a congenial spirit and friend of Clemens, was editor of the highly respected *Overland Monthly.* Harte and Clemens set a raw-boned and swaggering tone for western journalism of the time. Today if Bret Harte is remembered at all, it's because of his classic short story, "Luck of Roaring Camp."

In 1865 teenage brothers Charles and Michael de Young borrowed a twenty dollar gold piece from their landlord and published a tabloid handout, the *Daily Dramatic Chronicle* that was full of gossip and theater notices. It was the predecessor of the *San Francisco Chronicle.* Their father was a jeweler and dry goods merchant.

In 1887 U.S. Senator George Hearst, self-made millionaire, accepted the *San Francisco Examiner* as payment for a gambling debt. He gave it to his son "Willie"—William Randolph Hearst who wanted his own newspaper.

In 1895 Fremont Older was a crusading and hell-raising editor of the *Bulletin.* He was considered a tough newspaperman's newspaperman. He was a tireless fighter against civic corruption and a staunch defender of prostitutes.

Flamboyant, audacious, tough, controversial were descriptors for boy wonder Paul C. Smith. He became editor of the *Chronicle* in 1935 when he was 27. Under Smith, the *Chronicle* became known as the *New York Times* of the West, but circulation went south and *Time Magazine* referred to him as "an aging boy wonder." He lived in a showcase apartment on Telegraph Hill just below the summit and held parties there that included celebrities like Noel Coward and Clare Boothe Luce, who drank single malt scotch out of crystal tumblers and intermingled with *Chronicle* editors, reporters and copyboys. The apartment on Telegraph Hill is still there. Smith is not.

Herb Caen joined Smith's *Chronicle* in 1936 as a radio columnist but went on to become the man who reinvented San Francisco in his own image. Caen did not reflect San Francisco, San Francisco reflected Herb Caen's "Baghdad by the Bay" column. If you didn't read Caen's column you felt out of it.

When Scott Newhall took over as *Chronicle* editor in 1952 circulation was 170,000. The *Examiner's* was 350,000. Newhall revived a raucous San Francisco journalism practiced earlier by Clemens and others and turned the *Chronicle* into a frisky newspaper that was fun to read. When the sometimes prudish *Examiner* started a campaign to put tops on topless dancers in North Beach, Newhall editorialized: "The trouble with San Francisco is not topless dancers, it's topless newspapers."

The *Chronicle's* much-admired Stanton Delaplane was master of spare, boiled-down, whimsical sentences. He was a great prose stylist, none like him today. Herb Caen—himself not too shabby with words—likened Delaplane to Ernest Hemingway: "...he boiled down a sentence to its essence. The most hard-bitten editor couldn't find an ounce of fat to trim."

Cigar-chomping Bill Wren, who became city editor for the *Examiner* in the 1930s, went on to become a domineering, dominating and daunting managing editor. It was said that he ran the city, telling politicians and the police how to handle their jobs.

In 1944 Thomas Fleming founded the *Reporter*, then San Francisco's only Afro-American newspaper. He remained editor when the paper merged later with the *Sun* to become the *Sun-Reporter*. He ran a tight ship and got the news. A tough but sweet guy who had time for everybody.

Frances Moffat not only reported on the deeds and doings of San Francisco's socially elite for the *Examiner* and then for the *Chronicle*, but did so in a professional manner that positioned her subjects as an important force in the city's economic and philanthropic scene. She took the position that her society "beat" was the equal of any other on the newspaper—politics, business and financial, education, health, technology, arts and entertainment or sports. She was a hell of a good reporter.

Early on, women reporters were known as "sob sisters." But that put-down by their male compatriots didn't fly with conscientious women editors and reporters—among them Carolyn Anspacher of the *Chronicle* and Mary Crawford of the *Examiner*. Both hit the glass ceiling and broke through it.

One of the most interesting periods in the San Francisco newspaper scene was when William Randolph Hearst came to town to take over the *Examiner*. Competition was fierce. Here's how the city's newspaper wars played out.

William Randolph Hearst, an only child, was a wayward student and was expelled from Harvard for sending engraved silver chamber pots to his professors. He landed a job as a reporter on the *New York World*. Then in 1877 when he was twenty-three, his father gave him a birthday present—the *San Francisco Examiner*. Not a bad present for a 23-year-old kid. Hearst plunged into the *Examiner* like a kid into a swimming hole. He was inspired by the style of journalism he saw at Joseph Pulitzer's *New York World*—personal, vindictive, frequently lurid and above all, powerful. He began hiring the best journalists he could find, among them Samuel Langhorne Clemens (Mark Twain), Ambrose Bierce, Stephen Hart Crane, Richard Harding Davis and even Jack London. A fierce competitor, Hearst was the inspiration for the Orson Welles classic film, *Citizen Kane*, which Hearst had tried to stop.

"W R", as he was called in staff memos, built a formidable publishing empire. At its peak there were twenty-eight newspapers, eighteen magazines and several radio stations and movie companies. Hearst was known for showmanship and style that incorporated an iron hand in a not-necessarily velvet glove. In a book of reminiscences—*Skyline*—journalist-biographer Gene Fowler said "William Randolph Hearst was the kind of man who would call upon the north wind to snuff out a candle."

Hearst died August 14, 1951 at eighty-eight in the Beverly Hills home he shared with his mistress, actress Marion Davies.

The Poets of Angel Island

Poetry carved into wall in the Detention Barracks for men at Angel Island
PHOTO: WIKIMEDIA COMMONS

CHINESE BEGAN immigrating to San Francisco in large numbers soon after gold was discovered in California in 1848. They were badly treated although they helped build the transcontinental railroad, many Napa and Sonoma wineries, and labored in the state's light industries. Angel Island, the California State Park in San Francisco Bay, was used as an immigration detention site from 1910 to 1940 for Chinese (as well as other minorities) who journeyed from their motherland to build a new life in California. They were awaiting the outcome of health examinations and final disposition of their quest for immigration.

Long after the old Chinese detention barracks had been closed a park ranger found Chinese characters inscribed on the walls. In their frustration, the detainees, many of whom spent months and even years there, carved personal poems on the walls. More than 135 have been recorded. The poems are written in the Chinese classical style and provide a vivid reminder of a sad chapter in Chinese-American history.

Here is an example:

> *My parents are old; my family is poor.*
> *Cold weather comes; hot weather goes.*
> *Heartless white devils,*
> *Sadness and anger fill my heart.*

———•·•———

Fatso and Frida

Portrait of Frida Kahlo and Diego Rivera, 1932
PHOTO: WIKIMEDIA COMMONS

DIEGO RIVERA, the internationally-renowned and controversial Mexican artist, accepted a commission to paint a landmark giant mural at the Golden Gate International Exhibition that took place on San Francisco's Treasure Island in 1939-1940. It was part of the Exhibition's "Art in Action" project. The mural was called *Pan American Unity* and Rivera created the 1,800 square-foot *fresco*, enriched by not-too-obscure symbolism, as thousands of fair goers watched him work. It featured "The marriage of artistic expression of the North and South on this continent," he said at the time. *Pan American Unity* consisted of ten giant panels. One featured the artist, his back turned to his ex-wife, Frida Kahlo (herself an internationally known artist), as he faced his lover, movie star Paulette Goddard who was married to another Hollywood legend, Charlie Chaplin, also depicted in the Rivera mural. Later, when asked why he painted himself holding the actress's hand, he replied, "To promote closer Pan-American relations."

Frida Kahlo was Rivera's third wife. After their divorce in Mexico, he re-married her in San Francisco. They remained together, but lived in separate but adjoining houses in Mexico City until she died in 1954 at forty-seven. A volatile woman, Kahlo met Rivera in 1922 when she was a young student at the National Preparatory School in Mexico City and he already a celebrated artist painting his first mural there. She contrived to meet him by declaring to her school friends that she wanted to have a child by the famed artist, and referred to him as "Old Fatso." It worked, and within the month the couple began courting and then married in 1929. Kahlo herself became a brilliant painter in the surrealist mode. She had a series of physical problems and mishaps that left her partially disabled, nevertheless she was a powerful partner for Rivera and their relationship was tempestuous. The charismatic Rivera was equaled by Kahlo in physical appetites. His lifelong habit of romantic involvement with women was matched by her many affairs with men—including Leon Trotsky, the Russian communist and political refugee, then exiled in Mexico—and with women, including several movie stars.

Rivera had warm associations with San Francisco and found it to be a fascinating bohemian city and a source for major commissions for his work.

In 1940 Timothy Pflueger, well-known San Francisco architect and an organizer of the Golden Gate International Exposition, invited Rivera to create the *Pan American Unity* mural. When completed it was to be installed in a new library building planned for construction on the grounds of San Francisco Junior College of which Pflueger was the principal architect. But in 1941 U. S. entry into World War II halted most construction projects and a permanent site for the mural was considered nonessential for the time being. Rivera, a life-long communist, until a few months before his death in 1957 when he became a Catholic, differed with Josef Stalin on ideological matters and was subjected to constant controversy. In the U.S. many considered Rivera not just politically incorrect but a wild-eyed radical. He enjoyed his self-publicized and well-deserved reputation as a womanizer. This was fueled by the depiction of Paulette Goddard and Charlie Chaplin in the mural and by accounts in his autobiography of his first mistress—he aged thirteen, she, an 18-year-old American school teacher in Mexico. (There were even dark mutterings about cannibalism in his student days.) In any case, the mural was kept in storage until Rivera's death in 1957. Later the San Francisco School Board approved a proposal to house the mural in the foyer of City College of San Francisco's performing arts theater where it was finally installed in 1961.

When Rivera came to San Francisco to paint *Pan American Unity* it was not the first time he had been to the city. San Francisco had embraced him earlier in 1931 when he journeyed to the U.S. to undertake a series of important commissions. One was for the Pacific Stock Exchange, the other for the California School of Fine Arts, now the San Francisco Art Institute. During this earlier visit Rivera cut a wide, exciting swath through social and bohemian circles of the city. He and his wife Frida were photographed on their arrival by Southern Pacific train by the young photographer Ansel Adams. Adams's photograph showed Rivera with his ever-present cigar, scowling under a broad brimmed hat. The pair's arrival was covered by the dailies. The lumbering, rumpled—some said—bullfrog-like artist with the bulging eyes, was well-known in San Francisco.

When he returned ten years later to paint his *Pan American Unity*, Rivera lived on Telegraph Hill at 42 Calhoun Terrace and partook of the heady pleasures of nearby North Beach. Then, perhaps tiring of bohemian life in San Francisco, he sent for Frida Kahlo, whom he had earlier divorced. Within weeks she joined him. Early in December of 1940 they went to City Hall, acquired a license and were remarried. But the famous couple returned to a state of marital bliss only briefly. Frida returned to Mexico City before Christmas. She had exacted a draconian set of pre-marital conditions—she would support herself, she said. He would pay half of all household expenses. There would be no sex between them.

Born in 1886 in Guanajuato, Mexico, Diego Rivera studied traditional European artistic styles in school. By the time he was sixteen he had also absorbed the traditions of Mexican folk art, was combining them with European classicism and had become a talented and skillful painter. He visited Spain and studied the works of Goya, El Greco and Brueghel in Madrid's El Prado. Later he lived in Paris, became a friend of Pablo Picasso and was influenced by the cubism of the time. He also visited Italy and studied *fresco* painting techniques employed by the Renaissance masters. It was these *fresco* techniques that he employed for his major murals.

Returning to Mexico he became influenced by the Mexican Revolution of 1910-1917 and the Russian Revolution that followed. Rivera and other Mexican artists, notably David Alfaro Siqueiros, Jose Clemente Orozco and Rufino Tamayo, became committed to a turbulent public art that they displayed in grandiose detail on the walls of public buildings across Mexico. They explored what they believed was a direct artistic line flowing from prehistoric Mexican rock paintings and sophisticated murals of the Mayans, to their own large public murals depicting Mexico shown in allegory and symbolism.

Rivera idealized the Mexican Revolution for its people and gave them something to proud of. He became a leader of a cultural revolution there and in the process became internationally famous.

In 1930 he brought his bold art to North America. The first of his San Francisco commissions was for a large staircase mural in the San Francisco Stock Exchange Tower at 115 Sansome Street. The building opened in 1930 and served as the administrative wing of the San Francisco Stock Exchange. The tenth and eleventh floors housed a luncheon club from 1930 to 1987. Today that same space is devoted to the City Club, still basically a members-only luncheon establishment. The centerpiece remains a Diego Rivera staircase mural, *Allegory of California*, which he completed in 1931. One figure, the earth goddess, was modeled on then tennis star Helen Wills Moody. Other figures

rendered by Rivera were Peter Stackpole, son of sculptor Ralph
Stackpole, whose work still decorates the building, James Marshall,
who discovered gold at Sutter's Mill in 1848 and horticulturist Luther
Burbank. Rivera's selection to paint the *fresco* mural in this citadel of
capitalism, his first in the U.S., was controversial.

That same year Rivera undertook another mural in San Francisco.
It was done for the California School of Fine Arts, now the San
Francisco Art Institute at 800 Chestnut Street. It is located in a high-
ceilinged gallery and covers the upper two-thirds of an interior wall.
Called *The Making of a Fresco Showing the Building of a City*, it is divided
into three vertical sections by a *trompe l'oeil* wooden scaffolding that
frames an urban construction site. In the center Rivera painted himself
sitting on the scaffolding, his broad backside to the viewer, holding a
paintbrush and palette. At the time, a writer for a local arts publication
said "I would suggest his (Rivera's) predominant characteristic is a
conspicuous showmanship. He is the P. T. Barnum of Mexico."

When he finished these two murals he stayed several weeks in
the house of art patron Mrs. Sigmund Stern in Atherton. There he
painted a small mural in a shallow alcove in an outdoor dining area.
The mural depicts three children—Mrs. Stern's granddaughter Rhoda,
Rhoda's friend Peter, and Diaga, the child of the estate's gardener. It
now hangs in Stern Hall at the University of California in Berkeley.
Other miscellaneous works of Rivera can be found in museums and
private residences in the San Francisco area.

In 1932 the prolific Rivera created a large mural in the Detroit
Institute for the Arts and in 1933 began one in New York's Radio City
for the Rockefeller family. Because it depicted Russia's communist
leader Nikolai Lenin, it was destroyed. Later Rivera re-created it in
Mexico City's Palace of Fine Arts. In the wake of the scandal caused by
the Radio City mural, the artist painted a series of *frescos* in New York's
New Worker's School. He did these without fee.

Shortly before her death in 1954 Frida Kahlo had this to say about
her errant husband. "I suppose everyone expects a very feminine report
about him, full of derogatory gossip and indecent revelations. Perhaps

it is expected that I should lament about how I have suffered living with a man like Diego. But I do not think that the banks of a river flow, nor does the earth suffer because of the rains, nor does the atom suffer for letting its energy escape. To my way of thinking, everything has its natural compensation."

The final word on Diego Rivera is better left to his fourth and last wife Emma Hurtado. Just before his death in 1957 from complications of cancer of the penis, she said "The more he lives the greater grows the desire for collectors to buy his paintings. It is no longer a question of what he says or does, or what the world thinks of him. He is already a classic and his greatness insures him against everything."

———•◦•———

PART THREE

The Western Edge

SAN FRANCISCO is an historic enclave much like a small Mediterranean city—especially its North Beach neighborhood—that sits on the western edge of the continent. "Western" is an important word here. It defines the city and its state of mind. San Francisco has a western sensibility, a western style, a western ambience, and a western "edginess"—if you will. It's a non-conformist city with a rakish bohemian culture and panache that has always provided a sense of creative possibility.

Boy Wonder Paul C. Smith

WHEN I WAS A WIDE-EYED, somewhat bewildered young reporter for the *San Francisco Chronicle*—a long way back in the newspaper's pre-Hearst history—the editor was Paul C. Smith, a brash, flamboyant and controversial, "boy wonder." Smith, who lived in an extravagant, two-story apartment on the Greenwich steps just below Coit Tower, became editor of the *Chronicle* in 1935 when he was twenty-seven. He was the youngest editor of a major metropolitan daily in this country.

Smith was born in Seattle in 1908 and was largely on his own from the age of ten when he repeatedly ran away from boarding school. Before he was twenty-one he had been a ranch hand, lumberjack, apprentice seaman and a vice president for a San Francisco bank. He became financial editor of the *Chronicle*, then later its editor and general manager.

Enterprising and cocky, Smith ran the *Chronicle* with an expansive, in-your-face bravado that gained him an international reputation. In 1938 on the eve of World War II he went to Europe with his mentor, the former U.S. President Herbert Hoover, where he interviewed Neville Chamberlain, Anthony Eden, Hitler, Goering, Goebbels, Mussolini and other international figures of the time. He sent incisive reports back to the *Chronicle* editorializing that much of the globe would soon be engulfed in World War II. A year later, after he had mediated and settled a particularly acrimonious warehouse strike, more than 40,000 San Franciscans petitioned him to run for mayor. He declined saying he saw war in the future and would want to get into it.

The controversial Smith, always elegant but with a raw-boned western-ness about him, was welcomed in San Francisco's finest drawing rooms and the hallowed halls of Nob Hill's Pacific Union Club. But

Paul C. Smith, formal studio portrait
PHOTO: AUTHOR'S COLLECTION

what he enjoyed most was entertaining legendary visitors to the city like Dorothy Parker, Noel Coward and Clare Booth Luce and mixing these luminaries with locals such as labor leader Harry Bridges and rank and file editors and reporters from the *Chronicle*. Even the copyboys were invited. Many of these affairs ended with the entire troop walking down Telegraph Hill to finish off the night at one of the neighborhood saloons. Smith frequently wandered North Beach in those days, sometimes with buddies like William Saroyan and John Steinbeck.

I recall being invited to Smith's Telegraph Hill aerie several times when I was a copyboy and later as a lowly and expendable "cityside" reporter. At one of these events Smith introduced me to a youthful man named Richard Tregaskis.

"Richard Tregaskis," I exclaimed, recognizing the name of the author of the World War II book about the U.S. Marine Corp called *Guadalcanal Diary*.

"Yeah. Are you one of those assholes who joined the marines after reading my book?" he asked.

And, of course I was.

When Smith became editor of the *Chronicle* in 1935 and until the early fifties, there were four daily newspapers in San Francisco—*Call-Bulletin*, *News*, *Examiner* and the *Chronicle*. The *Chronicle* and the *Examiner*, both morning newspapers then, were slugging it out for circulation dominance. Under Smith, the *Chronicle* was emphasizing international news and opinion.

When the U.S. entered World War II, high-profile Smith received a commission as a Navy lieutenant commander. He resigned the commission and enlisted in the Marine Corps as a private, was later re-commissioned as a marine second lieutenant, saw considerable combat in the Pacific and was awarded the Silver Star. When he returned to the *Chronicle* at the war's end he loaded the paper's editorial staff with former marines as I was—albeit a bit later in a peacetime Marine Corps.

In the Smith days copyboys came from Harvard, Yale, Princeton and Stanford, and were on a fast track to becoming big-time reporters and editors. Some of them did and were known derisively by those on other San Francisco newspapers as "Smith's Whiz Kids."

Under Smith the *Chronicle* was widely recognized as the *New York Times* of the West but gradually the circulation diminished and *Time Magazine* referred to him as an "aging boy wonder."

The *Chronicle* was solidly (some said "boringly") "Responsible and Republican" but the bitter circulation rivalry with the *Examiner* eventually did Smith in with the ownership—heirs of the founding de Young family—and he left in December 1951.

Within a year he surfaced in New York where he became head of the Crowell-Collier publishing empire. But success was not to be his. He fought a rear-guard battle at Crowell-Collier which ended in the closure of *Collier's* magazine and a little later *Women's Home Companion* and the *American Magazine*. Those of us *Chronicle* alumnus who had joined him in New York packed our bags and headed for home.

After a period of drift, Smith moved to Big Sur to write his autobiography, *Personal File*, now out of print. During the Big Sur days I was one of many past tense *Chronicle* "whiz kids" who visited him there. On one occasion he let me read part of his manuscript. One passage about his days in New York with Crowell-Collier, stated "I posted one of my favorite aphorisms on my desk for all in the stream of visitors to contemplate: 'A Peacock Today; a Feather Duster Tomorrow.'" That evening as we discussed his life and career over heavy tumblers of scotch unencumbered by water, Smith said "I believe success is a journey; not a destination." I still like that better than the one about the peacock and the feather duster. Smith was an enigma. He was well aware of the notoriety and cult of personality that enveloped him and he enjoyed it and fed off it. His circle of friends included the literati, movie stars, politicians, tycoons, generals, enlisted marines. He moved in this constellation with a swagger and a fierce masculinity masked by a self-deprecating candor which, in reality, boosted him into an even higher stratosphere of celebrity. In 1976, long plagued by ill health, Paul Smith died at the age of sixty-seven in a convalescent home. He lived his life with zest and flamboyance, the afterburners roaring.

———•·•———

Herb Caen and his Item Smasher

San Francisco Chronicle columnist Herb Caen in his office, 901 Mission Street, San Francisco, California in the '90s
PHOTO: NANCY WONG / WIKIMEDIA COMMONS

DO YOU REMEMBER HERB CAEN? Well, if you're of a certain age and love San Francisco without question, you will remember the *San Francisco Chronicle* columnist who died in 1997. If you are a new and youthful San Franciscan or a visitor, the name may not resonate with you.

Pulitzer Prize-winning Herb Caen, who wrote a column about the "glitterati" and just plain folks who had stories to tell—large and small—worked the city. He liked to hang out in North Beach. His favorite saloons were Capp's Corner, the Washington Square Bar &

Grill and Enrico's over on Broadway. Caen would scratch around those joints and others around the city, for news tips that he then put into what he called his "item smasher"—a file of news and ephemera being considered for his next day's column. He called the column "Baghdad by the Bay" and it was considered required reading if you really wanted to be a city insider.

Caen could make or break a restaurant, a building project, or a politician. He was the Walter Winchell of San Francisco. Everyone wanted to be named in his column. It was a sign that you had arrived. You had stature.

Herb Caen could be prickly—a difficult but nice guy. But here is something you might not know about him. It may come as a surprise. Herb picked up his own tab. He paid the bill. And sometimes he paid yours too.

Stanton Delaplane and Irish Coffee

Stanton Delaplane and unidentified officer on cruise ship
PHOTO: AUTHOR'S COLLECTION

NORTH BEACH HAS ALWAYS ATTRACTED writers and many have lived here. They were inspired by the neighborhood's *la dolce vita* and understood the necessity of having pleasurable restaurants, bars and coffeehouses nearby. This is the story of one such writer, a reporter named Stanton Delaplane who, until his death in 1988, lived and worked in the neighborhood. Some of us called him "our esteemed writer in residence."

Delaplane wrote a column for the *San Francisco Chronicle*. He could say more in 600 words, say it better and with more style, than anyone I have ever known. Short, simple sentences sputtered deceptively across the page. Delaplane mistrusted most adjectives, but he liked verbs that gave his stories a compelling stop-and-go rhythm.

If you have ever enjoyed an Irish Coffee, you probably have Stanton Delaplane to thank. Years ago an old Lockheed Constellation ferrying a bunch of newspaper people to Rome to cover Holy Year celebrations blew an engine over the Atlantic and was forced to land for repairs at Ireland's Shannon Airport.

The first thing Delaplane and his chums did after the airplane made its shaky landing, was to head for the bar. It was a cold night and the bartender made them Irish Coffees—strong coffee and Irish whisky with a float of good Irish cream on top. At that time Irish whisky had scant sale outside the mother country. Later, back at the *Chronicle*, Delaplane wrote about the Shannon Airport bar and about Irish Coffee, and got a lot of mail asking how it was made.

One day he was sitting at the bar of the Buena Vista saloon at the foot of Hyde Street. He said he stared moodily out at the thin line of fog creeping under the Golden Gate Bridge and began thinking about Irish Coffee. Casually, he showed the late Jack Koeppler, owner of the B.V., how to make it.

"We couldn't get the cream to float. Irish cream is a lot thicker than ours. So we whipped it up a little, floated it on top and it tasted pretty good."

Irish Coffee took off. Delaplane continued to write about it in his column and soon Irish Coffee was an institution of sorts. The Irish whisky distillers were ecstatic. Delaplane told me that several years later he was in Dublin and received word that a group of distillers wanted to see him.

"They took me to a fancy old place with great carved walls and inlaid paneling, got me a bunch of sea-fresh oysters as a starter, and then one of them said 'Now, Mister Delaplane, what would you think if we put out a wee bit of a drink made with Irish whisky, a bit of soda and a slice of lemon? We'll call it the Leprechaun. Do you think it will sell?'"

"I don't know," said Delaplane. "In fact, I really don't know why Irish Coffee sells."

When he told them this he could see the group of distillers drawing back in disbelief. "They were thinking 'This guy knows how to do it, but he won't tell us his secret.' Anyway, they put out the Leprechaun and it dropped dead," said Delaplane.

When the impeccable prose stylist traveled, his widely syndicated *Chronicle* column "Postcard" reached millions of readers. He was the suave but kooky international traveler: He once journeyed to Mexico to find the head of Pancho Villa which had somehow become separated from the rest of the revolutionary general. But when at home in North Beach he wrote about dealing with the refrigerator repairman, trying to coax a kitten down from a tree, and his penchant for dipping into the cooking sherry.

He also wrote about North Beach. This is from his last published column. It was called "The Best News Came from North Beach."

"I walked in North Beach to sharpen my wits. The best cops drew North Beach. The restaurants spread a good table for them-as they did for reporters. Delicatessens sold 27 kinds of sausage—each one better than the last. A vinegar shop sold 50 flavors. There was a store where I bought fresh pasta. A French bread bakery where we stopped at four in the morning for a hot crusty loaf. The days were full of sun."

Stanton Delaplane was also a brilliant newspaper reporter whose stories frequently had a comic twist. In 1942 he won a Pulitzer Prize for a series of *Chronicle* articles he did on several counties along the California-Oregon border that half-seriously sought to establish a 49th state.

Delaplane usually began his columns at eight or nine in the morning, wrote slowly on his old Olivetti and carefully polished and re-polished. He was my neighbor on Telegraph Hill where he lived with his wife Laddie Marshack. At noon he made his way down to the Washington Square Bar & Grill at 1707 Powell Street, where he sat at his usual table, number 18, with a martini straight-up, and continued to re-polish the column with a big, black reporter's pencil, a soft-leaded Alpha 245. Awhile later a *Chronicle* messenger picked up the column and took it back to the paper.

"I write fast enough," he told an interviewer once. "It is getting at it that frays a man's nerves like an old shirt collar. Actually, it's something like barbecuing a steak. It is not the time on the fire. It is all those turns in the marinade; the loving touches with the fork and brush."

When Delaplane died, Ed Moose, then proprietor of the Washington Square Bar & Grill, decided to memorialize table number 18 by mounting a small brass plaque engraved "Reserved for Stanton Delaplane." One noon, several of us

Irish coffee
PHOTO: ERNEST BEYL

gathered for the ceremony. There was one place setting on table 18 and a stemmed glass with a martini straight-up. Overcome by nostalgia I picked up the glass, proposed a short toast, then downed the contents in one gulp. It was water. Delaplane would have liked that. It would have made a good column. Delaplane gave me his old Olivetti. I had it bronzed. Today it hangs on the wall in my apartment.

———•———

North Beach Poetry Renassaince

Kenneth Rexroth (right) reads poetry to jazz in a North Beach club
PHOTO: FRED LYON

KENNETH REXROTH led what is now termed San Francisco's Poetry Renaissance, and by most accounts must be considered a towering Northern California poet. Erudite, outspoken and highly influential, Rexroth vented his considerable poetic fury at war and the evanescent nature of a life unfulfilled. Overlooked for some time, his collected works have been republished.

How many went to work for Time?
How many died of prefrontal
*   lobotomies in the Communist Party?*
How many on the advice of
*   their psychoanalysts, decide*
A business career was best after all?

Although Rexroth was present at the dawn of the counterculture Beat Generation movement in the 1950s and served as its drumbeater and catalyst, he did not consider himself a part of it. In the introduction to the volume of his complete works, Sam Hamill recounts that when asked if Rexroth considered himself a Beat poet, he replied "An entomologist is not a bug."

Not for your how-to-do-it, hunting and fishing magazines is this bold and highly personal recollection:

I *realize as I*
Cast out over the lake
At thirteen thousand feet—
I don't know where you are.
It has been many years since we
Married and had children
By people neither of
Us knew in the old days.
But I still catch fish with flies
Made from your blonde pubic hair.

———•·•———

Allen Ginsberg and Howl

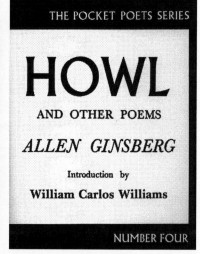

Allen Ginsberg, 1979
PHOTO: HAND VAN DIJK / ANEFO /
WIKIMEDIA COMMONS

Howl and Other Poems by Allen Ginsberg
PHOTO: AUTHOR'S COLLECTION

PERHAPS THE CONCEPT OF NORTH BEACH poets was best illustrated by the Beats—the 1950s group that included Jack Kerouac, Allen Ginsberg, Gregory Corso and Bob Kaufman, to name a few. The Beats merged with a group that Kenneth Rexroth, poet and counterculture spokesman, identified as the San Francisco Renaissance Poets, the most well-known of whom is Lawrence Ferlinghetti, now retired proprietor of City Lights Booksellers and Publishers.

On a history-making evening, October 7, 1955, five poets—Allen Ginsberg, Michael McClure, Gary Snyder, Philip Whelan and Philip Lamantia—appeared at San Francisco's Six Gallery and read their poetry. Ginsberg read *Howl,* which was soon to become the Beat anthem. Kerouac was there cheering him. Later that night Ferlinghetti sent Ginsberg a telegram offering to publish *Howl,* which he did. *Howl,* number four in the City Lights Pocket Poets Series, was printed in England and when it came into San Francisco, U.S. Customs and Immigration officials seized it. Ferlinghetti and Shigeyoshi Murao, the manager of City Lights, were promptly arrested by San Francisco police. The ACLU posted bail, Ferlinghetti vigorously defended the poem, as did noted San Francisco defense attorney Jake Erlich, and after a much-publicized trial, Judge Clayton Horn ruled in favor of Ferlinghetti.

Those were heady days. Poetry was being read aloud in North Beach joints like the Cellar where it was recited to the accompaniment of live, improvised jazz. Rexroth said "If we can get poetry out into the life of the country, it can be creative. Homer or the guy who wrote *Beowulf* was show business. We simply want to make poetry a part of show business." And they did. Upper Grant Avenue became the haven for what *San Francisco Chronicle* columnist Herb Caen termed "beatniks." Small clubs and coffeehouses sprang to life like the Co-Existence Bagel Shop, The Place, The Coffee Gallery, 12 Adler Place, Vesuvio's and the Anxious Asp. They attracted disaffected students, "suits" out of uniform from the world of business and commerce and East Coast magazine editors who spread the fame of the Beats and of San Francisco's North Beach.

Lawrence Ferlinghetti
PHOTO: JOHN PERINO / *NORTHSIDE SAN FRANCISCO* AUGUST 2010

Lawrence Ferlinghetti:
The Intellectual Guerilla

SEVERAL YEARS AGO I met poet Lawrence Ferlinghetti in City Lights, his landmark San Francisco bookstore in the city's Bohemian North Beach neighborhood. City Lights, became a kind of clubhouse for writers of the Beat Generation in the 1950s. Today, it's a magnet for baby boomer tourists to San Francisco and also for their offspring who read Ferlinghetti and Beat Generation writers like Jack Kerouac, Allen Ginsberg and others.

I was at City Lights to interview Ferlinghetti for a magazine story I was writing about San Francisco. Well aware of his towering reputation, I was apprehensive about talking to him. Ferlinghetti is widely recognized as one of this country's greatest living poets. So perhaps I was intimidated from the beginning by this man who published Ginsberg's *Howl* and was busted for doing so.

These days Lawrence Ferlinghetti, poet, painter, pamphleteer, former Poet Laureate of San Francisco, and retired publisher and bookstore proprietor, strides through the streets of San Francisco's North Beach like a colossus and continues to rail as he always has at big government, big business, civil rights abuses and this country's pugnacious war stance. Now in his 90s he walks tall and straight, his pale blue eyes fixed on another orbit. He has a mesmerizing presence.

Once I was seated in his wedge-shaped, manuscript-cluttered office above the bookshop, this is how that interview went:

FERLINGHETTI: Where is your tape recorder?

INTERVIEWER: I'm sorry I suppose I should have brought it.

FERLINGHETTI: This would work better with a tape recorder.

INTERVIEWER: I'll bring one next time.

FERLINGHETTI: I don't have much time.

INTERVIEWER: Let's meet again and I'll bring my tape recorder. Meanwhile, let's talk for a while.

Ferlinghetti shrugs. He looks doubtful about this meeting.

INTERVIEWER: Can we discuss the role of poetry in society as you see it?

FERLINGHETTI: Do you mean the "roll" (r-o-l-l) or "role" (r-o-l-e)? The poet's role is not to roll over. The poet's role is to exhort and harangue and to defend our civil rights. Our civil rights are constantly being challenged. They are being eroded daily.

A series of long vertical panels draped along the façade of City Lights Booksellers and Publishers stated then: "Dissent Does Not Mean You Are Un-American." At this writing the panels read "Stop War and War Makers."

INTERVIEWER: Actually, what is the state of the poet in our society?

FERLINGHETTI: The usual.

INTERVIEWER: I take it you mean by the "usual" that most people only read poetry once in a while or don't read it at all.

FERLINGHETTI: Poetry and poets are on the sidelines. If you have the time it's okay to read Byron, maybe Shelley or Keats, but not a bunch of crazies.

INTERVIEWER: Well, who does read poetry these days?

FERLINGHETTI: Almost everything is threatened and repressed. In our colleges and universities all the professors talk about is—the process of poetry. They don't ask what it means. I give poetry readings at colleges and the idea of the readings is to get the listener HIGH. Oral poetry, which is just one kind of poetry, should get people HIGH. But everyone wants to know about the process—"how" you wrote something. No one cares about the content, just the process.

INTERVIEWER: Well, who reads poetry besides the poets themselves?

FERLINGHETTI: Maybe a token poet who is a professor; or a token professor who is a poet.

INTERVIEWER: Today what other kinds of poetry are there besides oral poetry?

FERLINGHETTI: There is documentary poetry. I am working on documentary poem now called *Americus*. It's modeled on Ezra Pound's *Cantos*.

INTERVIEWER: What do you think your legacy will be?

FERLINGHETTI: That's up to the professors to decide—if they are interested in the question at all. They are in the deep sleep of the well fed.

INTERVIEWER: There's a common idea that you are a Beat poet and were a member of the Beat Generation.

FERLINGHETTI: Of course not. I was a member of the last Bohemian Generation. I even wore a beret. I published the Beats. I published Allen Ginsberg until later when he went over to Harper and Row. By that time he had shot his bolt. Did you get that? He shot his bolt by that time.

INTERVIEWER: Let's not dwell on the Beats, but rather on some other ideas and opinions; about the community in which you live. What's good about it; what needs improvement?

FERLINGHETTI: Next time bring your tape recorder.

INTERVIEWER: Okay, I'll do that.

I rise to leave.

FERLINGHETTI: Sit down and read this.

He hands me The Argonaut, *a publication of the California Historical Society.*

INTERVIEWER: I was going to leave because you said you didn't have much time. I'll bring my tape recorder next time.

FERLINGHETTI: Sit down and read this.

The issue of The Argonaut *featured a profile of Lawrence Ferlinghetti. We sit silently as I read the entire, five-page profile.*

INTERVIEWER: You seem to be a very public person, yet also a very private one. Since what I plan here is a profile on you, what are you comfortable in telling me about your personal life?

FERLINGHETTI: Nothing.

INTERVIEWER: I knew you were going to say that.

FERLINGHETTI: *Who's Who* sent me a questionnaire once

to fill out about my life and I wrote across it "fuck you." They sent me another questionnaire. This time I thought I would give them a surrealistic answer. At that time I thought I was a surrealistic poet. So I wrote "I was born either in 1919 or 1920. Born either in Paris or New York, etc."

We sit and look at each other for a few minutes. I have run out of gas. I stand and am ready to make my exit.

INTERVIEWER: Thanks. I appreciate your time. Next time I'll bring my tape recorder.

FERLINGHETTI: Sit down.

Ferlinghetti reaches back into a cubby hole of the roll-top desk at which he is sitting and brings out what appears to be a greeting card. He turns to the desk, takes up a pen and writes on the card.

FERLINGHETTI: Here, this is for you.

The single-fold, black-and-white card depicts Rembrandt's 1655 drawing, "Abraham's Sacrifice." It shows an angel, one hand over Isaac's eyes, the other restraining Abraham from killing Isaac. Below the illustration Ferlinghetti has written "By Rembrandt and Ferlinghetti." In a cartoon bubble coming from the angel's mouth he has written "If you can't look him in the eye you can't kill him!"

I open the card. On the left panel he had written "Happy New Year!" On the right panel he has written "To the bombers who kill thousands from 20,000 feet. Lawrence Ferlinghetti."

Certainly Ferlinghetti is highly conscious of his standing as a poet-activist. I respect him for that. What makes him a great poet is not only his poetry. It is also his unshakable belief in the importance of the poetic voice and his confidence that poetry is capable of transforming the world. To use a term by Bruce Chatwin in defining French novelist and critic Andre Malraux, Ferlinghetti is an "intellectual guerrilla."

In his monumental *A Coney Island of the Mind* published in 1958 he writes about a setting where he was able to move from the passive to the active as a poet.

> *Who may cause the lips*
> *of those who are asleep*
> *to speak*

And in the same poem he tackles just what it means to be poet:

Constantly risking absurdity and death
whenever he performs above the heads of his audience
the poet like an acrobat climbs on rime
to a high wire of his own making

The Puckish Mister Gold

SAN FRANCISCO has more than its share of literary lights—not to mention lites. No need to dwell on past giants—Bret Harte, Jack London, George Sterling, Ambrose Bierce, William Saroyan, Kenneth Rexroth and Allen Ginsberg—to name a few who come to mind quickly.

The present landscape of heavyweights includes Lawrence Ferlinghetti, Michael McClure, Leo Litwak and Herbert Gold—again just to name a few who come to mind quickly. And Herbert Gold comes to mind more quickly since awhile back he published his memoir called *Still Alive.*

Gold is certainly one of our brightest literary lights and one of the most prolific—eighteen novels to date and dozens of short stories and essays in literary journals, popular magazines and newspapers to keep Google-eyed researchers busy for a while.

A long-time resident of Russian Hill, Gold ran away from his home in Cleveland, Ohio in 1941 when he was seventeen and headed west to San Francisco where he stayed for a short time in North Beach. As many runaways do, he returned home a changed person; he realized, he said, that San Francisco and Cleveland were not at all alike. He filed away the San Francisco experience for the future. Later, in 1957, he visited the city again, staying with his Columbia University friend Allen Ginsberg.

Herbert Gold moved to San Francisco permanently in 1960. With intellectual leaps and bounds he has been able to tip toe between the worlds of both the Beats—many of whom he knew well—and the Establishment, where he has staked out an easy-going Bohemian presence.

Gold's first novel, *Birth of a Hero*, was written in Paris where he went on a Fulbright Scholarship. It was published in 1951 and explored a fictional account of his Jewish childhood in Cleveland. Reviews were good for a first novel written by a 27-year-old kid.

In 1956 he published a picaresque novel, *The Man Who Was Not with It*, that captured the same rootless disaffection explored by Jack Kerouac in *On the Road* which was published that same year. Then followed a long burst of creativity that continues today.

Gold's novel *Fathers*, published in 1967, was praised widely. Critic Larry Smith called it "…a book as skillful and rich as Ivan Turgenev"— not insignificant praise.

As one would expect, Gold is a compelling storyteller and an easy, quick-witted conversationalist. As a keen observer of contemporary life and pop culture, he captures the emotional patterns of a time and place. Several of his books are set in San Francisco, largely in North Beach. For example his novel *A Girl of Forty,* published in 1986, details the loopy California lifestyle of Susan Read (who calls herself Suki, of course).

Herbert Gold has lived in a rent-controlled railroad flat on Russian Hill for more than fifty years. Recently, after greeting this interviewer he proceeded down his long narrow hallway like a proud docent in an esoteric museum. He paused to point out a watercolor by Henry Miller, a striking black and white photograph of Allen Ginsberg, several Haitian paintings and photos of his five kids by two former wives.

But the principal stop on the tour was the small, cluttered office where Gold pointed to a black Remington Standard typewriter—not a computer in sight—and said Luddite-like: "I've written a lot of books on this."

Herb Gold, 2015
PHOTO: ERNEST BEYL

And indeed, there were dog-eared copies of those books—including translations in Japanese, French, German, Dutch, Danish, Spanish and Chinese, and a pirated Asian edition of *Fathers*—all wedged onto sagging shelves above his desk.

The Gold interviews took place over several days in his apartment and in a nearby Chinese restaurant where he is well-known. He invariably dines out three meals a day, ranging from his Russian Hill digs to North Beach, to the Mission—and also up to Nob Hill and over to Pacific Heights, where he is a convivial member of the social elite and invited regularly into the drawing rooms of some of the city's most imposing family mansions and consulate residences.

Now 91, Gold obviously relishes conversation and the opportunity to observe and salt away his impressions. A puckish, dark-eyed, gray-bearded, compact man with an elongated head like a self-portrait of El Greco, Gold was easily recognized and approached on the short walk to lunch. He ran into his postman who was searching through a mail sack.

"Have you got the notification of my Nobel Prize in there? Gold asked him.

The mail carrier laughed and pretended to search further in his bag. It was an old joke between them.

*

INTERVIEWER: Let's see if we can clear something up right now. You knew the writers of the Beat movement. You hung around with them and your name is linked frequently with Allen Ginsberg. But you weren't then and aren't now a Beat writer, are you?

GOLD: That's true. Allen used to say "First breath, best breath." Another way of putting it is—first thought, best thought. It was Ginsberg's rationale for spontaneity and self-expression and sometimes it can be eloquent. Allen was eloquent. Kerouac, who wrote *On the Road* while on Benzedrine, could be eloquent too. But in his case first breath wasn't best breath. He intended *On the Road* to be spontaneous prose, but he did a lot of rewriting. Nevertheless, much of Beat writing is an explosion of expression. Spitting it out and letting it all hang out there. That was Beat.

I am all for spontaneity, but I want to communicate clearly with my readers. I like stories. I like to think about them and let them ripen, so I guide them and shape them. For me, first breath is only the beginning. But I am associated with the Beats because I was a contemporary and attended Columbia University in New York where the Beat movement got underway. I was a good friend of Allen Ginsberg whom I met at Columbia. I also knew Jack Kerouac who was there for awhile although I didn't especially like him. I thought he was full of himself and he could be unpleasant when he was drinking, which was most of the time.

INTERVIEWER: Can we revisit those Columbia years since they were so important in your development as a writer?

GOLD: Well, I was born and raised in Cleveland and went to Columbia in 1942, but I left and went into the army in 1943. Because my parents were Russian-Jewish immigrants, I was trained to be a Russian interpreter. The plan was for some of us to parachute into China to help the Russians fight the Japanese. But before this occurred the big bomb was dropped on Hiroshima and then the war was over. I got out of the army, got married and almost immediately had two kids. I was only twenty-one, a kid myself.

I went back to Columbia in 1946 and got a BA and an MA in philosophy and it was during that period that I met and associated with Ginsberg, Kerouac, William Burroughs and others. Allen was just nineteen or twenty when I met him. We used to hang out in the West End Bar near Columbia. He talked constantly about homosexuality and he couldn't understand why I was unwilling to experience the gay life. He was gay and I am decidedly straight.

One year Allen and I shared a Columbia literary prize for poetry. My poem was actually a long Beat-like poem about Cleveland. It began *"Euclid looked on Booty Bare…"* I was riffing on the Rockefellers and Standard Oil which started in Cleveland. Allen's poem was a tight lyric in the fashion of English, 17th Century poet Robert Herrick. Interestingly Allen went on to become a Beat poet. I did not. We went in opposite directions.

INTERVIEWER: What did you do when you got out of Columbia?

GOLD: I realized that I didn't want to go back to Cleveland. Fortunately I was awarded a Fulbright scholarship and went to Paris with my wife and kids where I was a grad student studying philosophy at the Sorbonne. While there I finished my first novel, *Birth of a Hero*. I had no agent so I just packed up the manuscript and mailed it to Viking Press. A couple of weeks later Saul Bellow whom I knew, knocked on my door unannounced and said that Viking, his publisher at the time, had asked him to visit me and to assure the editors that I had not plagiarized the book and that I might be interested in writing another one. Saul became a mentor to me. He was a great writer and a wonderful guy. Anyway, the book came out and I moved back to Cleveland. Then I decided to go to Haiti. I love Haiti and I've been there many times over the years.

INTERVIEWER: Why did you go to Haiti the first time and how do you explain the attraction it has for you?

GOLD: Well, for one thing, it's not Cleveland. I had met a young Haitian woman in Paris and she filled me with tales of this remarkable country. I had to go there. And predictably I loved it. Haitian art is wonderful.

I love the beauty of Haiti. I have wonderful associations with it and I've written about it a lot. My book *Best Nightmare on Earth: A Life in Haiti* was a best seller. I never met the infamous "Papa Doc" (Francois Duvalier, President of Haiti from 1957 to 1964, then President for Life from 1964 until his death in 1971). He was an extremely dangerous man. I wrote an article for the *New York Times Magazine* about him and how he was setting himself up to be proclaimed King. As a result I was banned from going back to Haiti. After "Papa Doc" died his son "Baby Doc" (Jean Claude Duvalier), became President for life. I received a postcard from Aubelin Jolieouer, Haiti's Minister of Information. It said simply "Herb, you can come home now." So I started going back.

While I was in Haiti Graham Greene visited. He had never been there before. I spoke French, and even Creole by this time. Someone told Greene I was a poor student and would make a good guide. He wanted to meet beautiful Haitian women. I introduced him to a very attractive woman from a Haitian dance troupe. He said she was a lesbian. He had just returned from Saigon and I think he was stoned. He bought me dinner at an expensive restaurant in a fine hotel. I volunteered to pay for drinks. By the time the evening ended he was drunk and had a huge pile of saucers in front of him signifying how many drinks he had. I was worried I wouldn't be able to pay the bill. But I think he was testing me. He paid and I never saw him again. As a result of his trip he wrote his novel *The Comedians*.

INTERVIEWER: You've lived in San Francisco for a long time.

You obviously like it here. Tell us about the attraction you have for San Francisco.

GOLD: I've loved San Francisco since I first ran away from Cleveland and came here as a kid. When I was in the army I visited here. Later I came out to San Francisco to see Allen Ginsberg. And in 1960 I moved here permanently. When I first moved here I was playing tennis on January 1 and getting a suntan. I think that says it all.

INTERVIEWER: Earlier you told us about your admiration for Saul Bellow? What other writers do you admire?

GOLD: I think Vladimir Nabokov was a magnificent writer. Kurt Vonnegut was a great friend of mine and I love his work. The last time he was out here, it must have been about 2003, we spent the day walking out in the Mission. I took him into Adobe Books and introduced him to the owners. During the conversation it came out that they were having trouble paying the rent. Kurt found a paperback edition of his great novel *Slaughterhouse Five*. He quickly drew a self-portrait on the inside front cover, signed it and gave it to them. Later they told me they sold it for enough to pay a month's rent on the bookshop.

INTERVIEWER: You look happy and healthy. What is your daily routine?

GOLD: I usually get up early and work awhile at my typewriter. Notice I said "typewriter." I don't own a computer, or a cell phone, or a TV, or even a car. I had a car but it was stolen awhile back and I may not bother to get another. Anyway, mid-morning I walk down to the Concordia Club on Van Ness and work out. Then I either hike back home or take the bus. Then I sit down and write again. Or sometimes I walk down to North Beach to Caffé Puccini and sit there and write. Actually, I like writing in coffeehouses. I'm able to stay focused on whatever it is I'm writing about unless I am with friends.

INTERVIEWER: You seem to be a social animal.

GOLD: Well, I'm not reclusive if that's what you mean. I entertain myself but I enjoy a bit of the social ramble. I like parties—gallery openings, readings, book events, things like that. But writing is my first love, my profession, my job and I'm conscious of what I believe is my responsibility to write and write well.

INTERVIEWER: Which of your books do you like best?

GOLD: I suppose it's my memoir. It's called *Still Alive*. It's about aging, endurance and memory and it's told partly through memoir. It deals with the concept that we are only here on earth temporarily although we tend to think we are immortal. William Saroyan made a wonderful comment about aging. He said "Everybody has got to die, but I always thought an exception would be made in my case." I suppose we all feel that way. If I have one problem (a good problem for me) it's that I'm healthy. Many of my contemporaries are either gone or not healthy. I no longer go to college reunions. I'm afraid to see my contemporaries. Apparently I chose my parents well. They both lived into their nineties. I plan to live to one hundred and ninety.

What consoles me about the inevitable end is the drive to make some kind of mark on the world that will live forever and that my children are imprinted with something from me. That's important to me. I have to leave that up to posterity but if some of the words I have written are useful or helpful or entertaining, they will live on. Maybe I will have done something that will leave a mark.

INTERVIEWER: Are you working on anything now?

GOLD: I am, but it's private.

———•———

Melvin Belli Esquire

Melvin Belli, 1967
PHOTO: WIKIMEDIA COMMONS

IN THE 1960s I operated a one-man PR business in San Francisco. I rented space in lawyer Melvin Belli's historic brick headquarters on Montgomery Street on the edge of North Beach, Belli and his attorneys occupied adjacent, two-story buildings at 722 and 728 Montgomery Street. That part of the Belli complex, 722 Montgomery, was the birthplace of Freemasonry in California and was built in the 1880s.

My fledgling PR operation was on the second floor of 722 Montgomery, right above the flamboyant lawyer's sumptuous office on the ground floor. Belli's office resembled nothing less than a Hollywood dream of the ultimate Gold Rush saloon—part bordello with velvet hangings and tufted, overstuffed leather couches. There was a long stand-up bar with a brass foot-rest running its length and a beveled, back-bar mirror. Belli's law books were stacked on shelves that climbed to the ceiling from which hung a crystal chandelier. Belli, who favored tailored suits with tight black jackets lined with crimson silk, worked conspicuously at an enormous partner's desk. Behind that desk, always piled with legal briefs, letters, newspapers and magazines, was another desk, an antique roll-top, its cubbyholes and drawers stuffed with the stuff of Belli's not inconsiderable adventurous life.

Multi-paned windows of this saloon-office looked out onto Montgomery Street. And, of course, San Francisco tourists and residents alike were free to look in those windows on the ground floor where the great Belli was frequently at his desk. Except for the year-end holiday season, Belli stuck newspaper and magazine clippings about his legal and other triumphs on those windows—facing outward to the sidewalk at eye level. During the holidays he did the same thing with Season's Greetings cards. So, while the Pisco Punches, which Belli favored as party drinks for the politicians, newspaper editors and reporters, socialites, movie stars and assorted oddballs, were raised in toasts to Belli indoors, others looked on from the sidewalk.

As I said in the forward to this book, San Franciscans have long had a fascination with larger-than-life characters who have contributed a sense of vigor to this Gold Rush city. Belli certainly was a character and he certainly contributed a sense of vigor. He was also a damned good, if melodramatic, attorney. I never faulted him for his theatrical Montgomery Street building or for his crimson-lined jackets. I wish we could bring back both the man and the building.

Of course, I tried to ape Belli in the furnishings of my own office, right above his. Potential PR clients seeking me out to burnish an image or promote a business, walked through a small flower-bedecked courtyard and turned left to go up the stairs to the second floor. If visitors did seek me out they found a heavy, black wooden door with a brass plaque with only my name on it. Low key! Belli had such a brass plaque on his door engraved *Melvin Belli, Esq.*

On entering my office, clients were greeted by a nubile young woman sitting at an old roll-top, not quite as elaborate as Belli Esq.'s below. A steep ladder-stairway led up to an overhanging loft where files were kept. Visitors sitting on the wooden armchair by the entrance awaiting an audience with the image-maker, enjoyed a kind of Marcel Duchamp version of my administrative assistant descending that steep staircase, usually in a mini skirt. It was good PR.

My office was furnished with second-hand this and that—old wooden library benches, bookcases from the Salvation Army store, an antique hat and coat rack with brass hooks, a beat-up partner's desk with worn, red leather inlaid on its top, an old adjustable, cast iron typewriter stand with claw legs and a worm-screw device to raise or lower it. On the stand stood an ancient, upright, open-sided Underwood typewriter. There was also an old apothecary chest from a long gone San Francisco pharmacy that had row after row of small drawers with brass labels that read POT PERMAN, LAP PUMICE, SULPHUR PRAECIP and my favorite, SAL LIMONIS (POISON). I thought the rawboned, San Francisco Gold Rush mood it attempted to evoke, to be—quite *Belli*.

This gaslight period, whorehouse splendor was highlighted by a three-by-five foot, beveled mirror mounted horizontally on the building's original brick wall to the left of my desk. I got the mirror in a junk shop on Upper Grant Avenue where I occasionally picked up such treasures. I learned later from another lawyer friend, Zeppelin Wong, that this very mirror had hung in a now-defunct bank on Grant Avenue in Chinatown. It had been presented to the bank by hopeful investors on the occasion of its grand opening. There, in simulated gold leaf, Chinese character brushwork proclaimed: *"Good Luck and Long Prosperity. Work Diligently and You Will Reap Plentifully."* At least that is what it said according to my friend "Zep" Wong. It was a splendid office.

As I think back now, I recall great and small dramas played out in the old Belli Building which I still miss. It was in that office that jazz avant-gardist Ornette Coleman and I planned a concert with full symphony orchestra to be held in the San Francisco War Memorial Opera House. The fact that it was stillborn did not lessen my pleasure in hanging out for a while with Ornette Coleman and his entourage. Belli himself came up one day to tell me about a jade mine in the foothills of California's Sierra Nevada that he wanted me to promote—a bad idea that later got me called up before the Securities and Exchange Commission. Belli defended me against allegations that I was improperly boosting a stock offering.

Then, there was the day when a stunning young woman burst into my office, moved around the partner's desk where I was sitting with my back to a tall, paned window. She clapped her hands over my ears to steady my wobbly head and kissed me full on the lips. For a climax she pulled open the window, stepped out onto the geranium box sitting on a narrow brick ledge and stood facing the street, arms akimbo, threatening to take a dive. She had come up from Belli's law office on the first floor. I never did figure out what that was all about.

As I write this the grand old Belli building is only a memory, a hulk surrounded by a plywood barricade, many of its windows boarded over, its roof collapsed right over where my partner's desk once sat.

———•—•———

From Madam to Mayor

Sally Stanford, 1952
PHOTO: SAN FRANCISCO HISTORY CENTER, SAN FRANCISCO
PUBLIC LIBRARY

IN HER BOOK *The Lady of the House,* published in 1966, Sally Stanford said "Madaming is the sort of thing that just happens to you—like getting a battlefield commission or becoming Dean of Women at Stanford University."

Mabel Janice Busby, who would become the idiosyncratic and famous madam Sally Stanford, was born in Oregon in 1903. Later she said she took the name because Sally was a good hooker name and she had seen a headline that read "Stanford Wins Big Game." Dysfunctional marriages finally led her to San Francisco where in the 1930s and 40s she operated a series of high-class parlor houses. The most famous of these was at 1144 Pine Street, furnished in Sally's favorite, elegant Victorian style. It featured a marble bathtub said to have belonged to actress Anna Held who enjoyed herself in it with milk baths.

Not exactly your shy and retiring madam, San Francisco columnist Herb Caen once referred to her operations as "Sally Stanford's School of Advanced Social Studies." There was also a short-lived marriage to Robert Gump, a member of the prominent Gump family that operated the renowned oriental art objects emporium of the same name. Sally Stanford finally retired in 1949 following numerous police shut downs. The next year she opened an opulent, Victorian restaurant called Valhalla across the Golden Gate in Sausalito. Its appointments reminded patrons of her former bordellos.

In 1962 she ran for a Sausalito City Council seat. After a spirited campaign in which she hammered home her political slogan "Live and Let Live," she finished third among the eight candidates. But not one to let adversity get her down, she repeatedly ran again and was finally elected. Then, having become a wise and even beloved figure, in 1976 Sally Stanford was elected Mayor of Sausalito. She died in 1982 at seventy-eight and flags were flown at half-staff in Sausalito.

———•—•———

Trout Fishing in America
and Richard Brautigan

RECENTLY I WAS THINKING ABOUT Richard Brautigan, the counter-culture novelist and poet who hung out in North Beach in the 1950s and 60s. It was North Beach artist Marcia Clay who brought Brautigan to mind when I talked to her a few months ago. But I'll get back to that. Although I barely knew Brautigan, I still miss him. He added a lot of color and verve to North Beach. He was a charming but irascible character. I saw him one day many years ago at Enrico's on Broadway. He was sitting at an outdoor table with friends. He wore his usual costume—outlaw western attire and a strange broad brimmed, black felt hat with an exaggerated high dome. The complete Brautigan package included a long, droopy handlebar mustache. I walked up to say hello and he stood, held out his hand for me to shake, tipped that kooky hat in a courtly manner, and we talked for a while. It was one of his good days. Frequently Richard Brautigan could be just the opposite of courtly—testy and irritable and off-hand to those he could not abide. The man had a habit of looking askew at the world, but I couldn't fault him for that.

Richard Brautigan was born in Tacoma, Washington in 1935 and grew up in the Pacific Northwest. He came to San Francisco in 1955 and associated with the Beats. He worked for a while with a local a messenger service while he surveyed the bubbling literary scene. In North Beach he met heavyweight poets like Michael McClure, Jack Spicer, Allen Ginsberg, Lawrence Ferlinghetti and Philip Lamantia.

Those were heady days. Poetry was being read aloud in North Beach joints like the Cellar where it was recited to the accompaniment of live, improvised jazz. Brautigan fit right in. He also recited his poetry on street corners and attended "Blabbermouth Night" at the

Place, a Beat club where you could read your work or just sound off about whatever was on your mind.

He bridged the gap between the Beats and the hippies. He was the hippies' chosen icon but he drank like a Beat. By this time his poetry was being printed here and there, and in 1964 he published his first novel, *A Confederate General from Big Sur*. The hippies loved it. It was outrageous and outlandish, a disjointed satire on the hippie life. Other novels, stories and poetry followed, including *Trout Fishing in America* and *In Watermelon Sugar*. These two and, *A Confederate General from Big Sur,* remain his best remembered books, although he wrote eleven novels. He received a grant from the National Endowment for the Arts and in 1966 and in 1967 he served as poet-in-residence for the California Institute of Technology.

He once wrote eight poems that were printed on seed packets, packaged and sold under the title *Please Plant This Book*. At that point his work was immensely popular and sold well. He spent some time in Japan where he was lionized, and then in the 1970s he moved to Montana and went underground.

By 1984 everything was crashing down around his ears. He felt neglected; his work was being ignored and he didn't know how to recapture the exhilaration he had felt when he was a young North Beach literary giant.

Let's have North Beach artist Marcia Clay pick up the story:

"I met Richard in the mid-70s in a North Beach club called Dance Your Ass Off, then at the corner of Columbus and Lombard. I was there one night when a guy I knew came over and said 'Tonight I am going to do you the biggest favor of your life.' He introduced me to Richard Brautigan and I danced with him. He danced like a cornstalk in the wind. Anyway, that led to a long friendship between Richard and me. We dated and he took me all over North Beach. He encouraged me with my painting and my writing. At that time he considered me his girlfriend but I wasn't sure I wanted to be that. It was clear that he had personal demons. He was a flawed but wonderful guy. Those were exciting days for me. Then he married and was later divorced and was out of my life.

"In 1984 I ran into him at Enrico's and he asked me to call him at his Bolinas hideaway in a few days. I called him on September 14, 1984 and he said he was writing again and wanted to read to me from his new book which he called *The Absolute End of Twilight,*" Marcia recalled.

It is widely believed that Marcia Clay was the last person to talk with Brautigan before he shot and killed himself with a 44-caliber weapon. Richard Brautigan once wrote "The act of dying is like hitchhiking into a strange town where it is raining and you are alone again."

Artist Marcia Clay

JAPAN HAS LONG DESIGNATED PREVIOUSLY UNSUNG HEROES or heroines in the arts or crafts as Living National Treasures. Perhaps there should be such a program in North Beach, certainly a hot bed of artistic creativity. My first nomination would go to Marcia Clay, artist who has lived in the neighborhood for more than thirty years.

I first met Marcia when she was a nine-year-old blonde brat who lived with her mother Anita in the Haight-Ashbury. Anita Clay Walker, a divorced single mother, was from Kansas City. A would-be writer, she was encouraged to come to San Francisco by the Kansas City novelist Evan Connell Jr. Anita picked up her three kids and her manuscripts and moved here. She married impresario John Kornfeld who presented concerts, recitals and other performing arts programs in San Francisco. Anita Kornfeld went on to publish two novels—the autobiographical *In a Bluebird's Eye* and the highly successful saga of a California winemaking family, called *Vintage*.

Marcia Clay came back into my life in the 1970s when San Francisco writer Alexander Besher and I worked together for a while. Besher lived near me in North Beach and wanted me to see his wife's oil paintings, watercolors and etchings. "What's her name," I asked? When he told me it clicked. I went to the couple's flat and wound up becoming a long-time admirer of Marcia and her work.

As I write this I glance from time-to-time to a nearby wall on which hangs a large self-portrait of Marcia that I purchased from her in 1979. It's an etching, a nude study called *Day Dreaming*. Marcia was born with cerebral palsy and that left her a somewhat canted, saucy look that comes through in this and other self-portraits. The disorder also gave her an assertive, slightly off-kilter gait, much like a two-year-old filly on her way to the starting gate that already knows she is going

Artist Marcia Clay
PHOTO: MUSH EMMONS

to win the upcoming race. Marcia Clay has that kind of buoyancy and confidence in herself. She's the eternal optimist with a broad and friendly smile. "I even enjoy my bad moods," she says.

In 1968 when she was fifteen Marcia skipped out midway in high school and went to France to study art at the *Ecole des Beaux Arts* in Brittany. When she returned to California a few years later she stopped in an art store to have one of her paintings mounted and framed, and she was "discovered" if you will, by a curator who gave her a one-person show at the de Saisset Museum in Santa Clara. She was seventeen and with her Paris *Ecole des Beaux Arts* classes added to her school record in San Francisco she was granted her high school diploma. And, to continue the horse race metaphor, she was off and running.

Today she has a Bachelor's degree in fine art and a Master's in creative writing, both from San Francisco State. In addition to her career as an artist, she was an English composition instructor at USF for more than ten years, worked for a time as a French translator and has found time to write two autobiographical novels now making the rounds of publishers. One concerns a young girl growing up with cerebral palsy; the other is based on her life as an art student in France.

Marcia's oils, watercolors and etchings have been featured in major galleries in France, on the East Coast and here in California. She has had one-person shows at the Robert Mondavi Winery in Oakville, Enrico's on Broadway and in the Telegraph Hill Gallery in North Beach.

She draws inspiration and themes largely from North Beach—street scenes with Chinese and Italian children, their mothers and grandparents. They interact in Washington Square, at outdoor markets, flower shops and playgrounds. Many of these have sly, humorous and frequently poignant, aspects. Other work depicts North Beach interiors, bedrooms, kitchens, restaurants and coffeehouses, with opulent figures brimming with life. Then there are her self-portraits—frequently edgy and sexy. "They all go through my perception of the world and of me as I see myself," she says.

Marcia's work sells well here and abroad. In reviewing an East Coast one-person show, the *Washington Post* described her as "a prodigious talent." Her paintings jump out at you with rich, deep color and movement. In my view her black and white etchings sizzle with what legendary photographer Henri Cartier-Bresson described as his seemingly random but exacting approach to the photographic art he identified as—"The Decisive Moment." But Marcia's work is not photographic. It reveals a distorted realism skewed by her highly selective imagination.

What keeps Marcia Clay in North Beach? "I love the cultural mix, the foreign influence, Italian, Asian," she says.

"I Was Stupid About Bob Dylan"

RALPH J. GLEASON, the perceptive music critic and social commentator who had a towering reputation, taught me much about blues, jazz, rock and other music and the environment that nurtured them. His *San Francisco Chronicle* column was required reading for anyone who paid attention to pop culture and the music it fostered and who wanted to dip themselves into that scene. Gleason once said to me: "It's happening where I am." And, I discovered that it usually was.

He made his declarative and dogmatic decree after I told him one day that on a given night I was going to a concert at the East Bay Concord Pavilion. "Because," I said "that's where it's going to be happening" and, I suggested rashly, that he would be well advised to turn up there as well.

As I recall, the same night I was going to the Concord Pavilion, Ralph was going to Chet Helms's Avalon Ballroom to hear Big Brother and the Holding Company with Janis Joplin.

Gleason, who died of a massive heart attack in 1975, could be puckish, obtuse and maddeningly self-assured. But that was okay with me. I idolized him.

Ralph occupied a world that encompassed all of popular culture. It seemed to me then that he was the nucleus and everything revolved around him, the whole incredible scene. His counsel was sought by a generation racing along to discover its own music. I was one who sought it. And with a dry suck on his ever-present pipe, he delivered his opinions (and his decrees) on jazz, pop, rock, folk and other musical styles and also on the sociological and generational factors that influenced it—freedom of speech and the freedom to exercise one's individual free spirit.

Gleason was born in New York City. He got hooked on jazz as a child when he came down with measles and a doctor told his family

Ralph J. Gleason in the press room at the Monterey Jazz Festival
PHOTO: MONTEREY JAZZ FESTIVAL ARCHIVES / JERRY STOLL

to keep him in bed in a darkened room. So he listened to the radio, particularly late at night. He heard strange sounds coming from the little black box. In his book, *Celebrating the Duke and Louis, Bessie, Billie, Bird, Carmen, Miles, Dizzy and other Heroes*, he stated "I lay there, wide awake, picking up those strange sounds in the night—Duke Ellington, Louis Armstrong, Cab Calloway, Earl Hines, Fletcher Henderson...and what I heard gave a thrust to my life which has never left."

When he attended Columbia University he continued his jazz education, visiting New York's 52nd Street and Harlem clubs and scouring dusty, secondhand shops for old 78 RPM recordings. He began publishing a newsletter called *Jazz Information* that was helpful to those smitten by the jazz bug as he was. Eventually he found his way to San Francisco and became a *San Francisco Chronicle* columnist.

Initially he covered only pop music and jazz. Later he broadened his mandate to include other musical subjects that interested him. He was an early champion of rock and appraised it thoughtfully when many others dismissed it with a shake of the head and a roll of the eyes. He defined the so-called San Francisco Sound and gave credibility to such early bands as Jefferson Airplane, Big Brother and the Holding Company, Quicksilver Messenger Service, Three Dog Night, Country Joe and the Fish and the Grateful Dead.

His *Chronicle* critiques and appraisals were masterpieces of interpretation of music and its role in shaping society. They could be vague and imperious, but they could also be clear-headed, and precise and compelling. In my view his musical taste was flawless.

Ralph J. Gleason and Jann Wenner founded *Rolling Stone*. And Wenner credited Gleason with giving the publication its eclectic focus. It was Gleason who named the long-running publication. He was instrumental also in the creation of the Monterey Jazz Festival. When the spark hit, that festival's founder Jimmy Lyons, sought advice from Gleason on how to make the event meaningful for both the artists and the audience. Today the Monterey Jazz Festival continues as a premiere jazz event.

Hundreds of liner notes for jazz and rock albums were written by Gleason, even for one by comic Lenny Bruce. The columnist hosted an award-winning National Educational Television show, Jazz Casual, which featured major artists and is still considered a milestone in the presentation of the music. Later, he became a vice president without portfolio (meaning he had a hand in everything) for Saul Zaentz's Fantasy Records. And Gleason and Zaentz produced a much-heralded movie about the music business called *Payday*. Many of Gleason's articles and essays of that period have been reprinted in anthologies and textbooks on music and American culture.

While Ralph moved all over San Francisco and beyond to review musical events he deemed important, he spent much of his time in North Beach hanging out at clubs like the Jazz Workshop, Sugar Hill, Basin Street West and El Matador because that's where much of the jazz scene was happening in those days. When the clubs closed for the evening he moved to Enrico's on Broadway for dialogue with the artists who played those clubs earlier in the evening—Duke, Dizzy, Miles, Lenny and other "heroes" as he called them.

When Gleason, known for keeping his ears open for anything, first heard Bob Dylan, he dismissed him as being of scant importance. A year later he publicly apologized for this. "I was stupid," he said, and then, still before much of the public adopted Dylan, he heralded the raspy singer as a new poetic voice and prophet for that generation.

When Gleason spoke he did so with complete conviction. His insightful comments and columns related blues, jazz, rock, pop, country, folk music and gospel to the popular culture with authoritative comments that drew on history, geography, sociology and psychology. Ralph's interests and knowledge were broad but he could be cold, precise and exacting.

On the other hand I was with him once at the Monterey Jazz Festival when Dizzy Gillespie came out on stage with his up-tilted, bent-to-heaven trumpet and blew a soft ballad out into the cold night air. When it was over Ralph had tears in his eyes. He took his music seriously.

Ralph J Gleason (far right) and Dizzy Gillespie (in cap) and unidentified woman in a box at the Monterey Jazz Festival
PHOTO: MONTEREY JAZZ FESTIVAL ARCHIVES / JERRY STOLL

In 1970, five years before his untimely death, Gleason wrote "Sometimes we are lucky enough to have one of these people like Miles, like Dylan, like Duke, like Lenny, here in the same world at the same time we are and we can live this thing and feel it and love it and be moved by it and it is a wonderful and rare experience and we should be grateful for it." From my perspective, we should add Ralph's name to that list. We should be grateful we had him with us at an important time in our lives.

How to Talk Dirty and Influence People

LENNY BRUCE, whom music critic and social commentator Ralph J. Gleason once described on a record jacket as "a verbal Hieronymus Bosch," loved to hang out in North Beach. In those days, back in the 1950s and 60s, the neighborhood had a loopy, funky edge to it. The night people were local night people; not only suburbanites and others looking for a San Francisco thrill on Broadway or Columbus.

Bruce took his comedy act to Anne's 440 club on Broadway and later to Enrico Banducci's hungry i where he had much success. Later, Bruce played the Jazz Workshop (also on Broadway) and was busted for obscenity in what became a national news event.

On another bad night, Bruce, who was staying at the Marconi Hotel on Broadway (everything happened on Broadway in those days), fell out of the window of his second floor room. He was severely injured when he hit the pavement. Some still say he was pushed.

Bruce was the bad boy of stand-up comedy. He was an audacious hipster, as we used that hip word in those days. In his act he unleashed long, complicated monologues on sexual hypocrisy, liberal pretense, racism, religion and government and business greed. Sounds just like today.

It would be interesting to have Bruce around now. The four-letter, ten-letter and twelve-letter words that shocked audiences then, are now read in many, almost-mainstream publications. On TV four-, ten- and twelve-letter words are used. HBO's Bill Maher frequently whips them out on his show. And George Carlin, the old dirty wordsmith himself, was still at it before he died in 2008. Bruce would probably not be amazed at how his once-*verboten* dialogue has taken over. More than likely, if he were with us today, he would say, "I told you so, (add ten-letter word)."

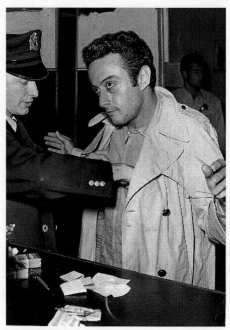

Newspaper press photo of Lenny Bruce being arrested, 1961
PHOTO: WIKIMEDIA COMMONS

In 1960 *Time Magazine* did a cover piece on the then new comics. Mort Sahl was on the cover. Inside were photos of Mike Nichols and Elaine May, Shelley Berman and a handsome Lenny Bruce—with a quizzical expression on his face and the index finger of his left hand pointing upward. He must have been invoking some higher authority. *Time* identified Bruce as "chief among the sick comedians" and said he "...whines and uses four-letter words." Apparently *Time* hadn't caught up with the ten- and twelve-letter words Bruce used in North Beach.

Lenny Bruce was a good friend of Enrico Banducci who told me "Lenny was a really sweet man. I gave him his first real club job. He told me he wanted to play the hungry i. I flew to San Diego to see him at some tiny club there. That night he was booed off the stage. But I liked what I heard and went backstage and offered him $250 a week to come to San Francisco and headline for me. The hungry i did well with Lenny. The audiences loved him."

I once asked Banducci if he could remember any routine from Bruce's hungry i days that I could use in a book. "Sure," Banducci said. "Lenny told a story about a guy who was out on parole and committed another crime and was going to wind up in the slammer again. The judge at his trial asks him if he has anything to say before sentencing. 'Well, judge,' he says 'I'd like to have my old cell back.' The judge asks why and the prisoner says 'I fixed it up with nice curtains and a fancy bedspread.' That knocked me out," said Banducci.

Throughout his career Bruce was hounded by authorities for so-called obscenity. His busts and subsequent trials were highly documented—especially the one in North Beach.

In 1961 he was appearing at the Jazz Workshop. A San Francisco police officer, saying he was there on an anonymous complaint, entered the club and arrested Bruce for liberal use of the ten-letter word. Interestingly, no customers had walked out of the Jazz Workshop on Bruce's act.

It was reported that the officer said to Bruce "We're trying to elevate this street. Our society is not geared to this word. How can you break it down?"

"By talking about it," Bruce replied.

He was taken to the station and booked for violation of Section 205 of the Police Code ("depicting or distributing obscene matter for the sake of prurient appeal.") He made bail and was back at the Jazz Workshop for the second show that same night. For this appearance he related his arrest and booking to his audience.

There was a trial in early March of 1962 and the ten-letter word that had pushed the police—or the unnamed complainant—to the limit, was exclaimed over and over. This pleased Bruce greatly. During the trial an impressive list of experts, including free-speech champion Ralph J. Gleason who, beside himself with enthusiasm, testified that Bruce's routines were not intended to be prurient but were simply echoing the long-proud tradition of social satire.

Someone even cited Aristophanes and Jonathan Swift. Bruce was acquitted.

Later, in the foreword to Bruce's autobiography *How to Talk Dirty and Influence People*, British critic Kenneth Tynan said "The point about Bruce is that he wants us to be shocked, *but by the right things* (Tynan's emphasis in italics), not by four-letter words, which only violate convention, but by want and deprivation which violate human dignity."

Gleason reported later: "So many taboos have been lifted and so many comics have rushed through the doors Lenny opened. He utterly changed the world of comedy."

In 1963 Bruce died of a heroin overdose in a Los Angeles hotel.

———•◦•———

The Buttoned-Down Comic

Photo of Mort Sahl and Ed Sullivan from an Ed Sullivan television special "See America with Ed Sullivan," 1960
PHOTO: WIKIMEDIA COMMONS

ANOTHER HUNGRY i ALUMNUS was Mort Sahl, a Southern California auto salesman. In 1953 he did a monologue about Senator Joseph McCarthy and talked about something called the McCarthy jacket. He said it was much like the popular Eisenhower jacket except it had "an extra flap to go over the mouth." It was Enrico Banducci who convinced Sahl—up to that time a coat and tie guy—to go on stage in chino pants, open, buttoned-down shirt and baggy sweater and to wave a folded newspaper at the audience as he skewered current politicians.

She Called Her Husband "Fang"

Phyllis Diller
PHOTO: ALLAN WARREN / WIKIMEDIA COMMONS

PHYLLIS DILLER didn't get around to trying stand-up comedy until she was thirty-seven. She quit her job with an Oakland radio station and in 1955 she opened at the Purple Onion on Columbus Avenue in North Beach. Her first line on stage was "I'm a housewife with five children. You may call me the girl with the seersucker tummy." She called her husband "Fang" and said "Nothing was happening in our marriage. I nicknamed our waterbed Lake Placid. I made varicose veins into an erogenous zone."

PART FOUR

The Paris of the Pacific

THE INDEPENDENT MAVERICKS who came to San Francisco wanted to get rich but they shared other desires as well. They sought good food and drink and good entertainment. They had money in their jeans, they expected the best and they got it. San Francisco was on its way to becoming the Paris of the Pacific.

North Beach, San Francisco, California, North East corner of Broadway and Columbus (1973). Carol Doda's Condor Club, Big Al's, Roaring 20s and Hungry I strip clubs, 1973
PHOTO: MICHAEL HOLLEY / WIKIMEDIA COMMONS

The Topless

WE ARE GOING TO DEAL HERE with the loopy North Beach history of bare breasts—the female variety, not beefcake. Many students of the art of ecdysiasm have been led to believe that it all started with an enterprising young woman named Carol Doda. Actually, women have bared their breasts in San Francisco—and especially in what has become North Beach—since the earliest days of this wacky, permissive city.

Right from the start, on the edges of Portsmouth Square, along the Embarcadero waterfront and the Barbary Coast and up on the slopes of Telegraph Hill, dancers, waitresses and conscientious amateurs—all with bare breasts—were commonplace. And while males ogled the women, their eyeballs didn't fall out of their heads in bafflement. Most had seen bare breasts before.

And so it went, down through the years.

Certainly, in modern times, Carol Doda led the way—that is, uncovering her breasts—and launched the topless craze that swept San Francisco and the nation back in the 1960s. But Gayle Spiegelman, billed as the "Topless Mother of Eight," and Yvonne D'Angier, the "Persian Kitten," were not far behind.

Carol Doda and her Swimsuit

CAROL DODA, who danced topless on a white piano in the Condor Club at Columbus and Broadway in the sixties, reinforced the racy reputation San Francisco has enjoyed since the days of the Gold Rush. I use the word "enjoyed" since the city has always been proud of being naughty as well as nice. Carol was the first topless star and her silicon-enhanced self was unforgettable. Soon the topless craze had swept around the country.

It's invigorating to live in a city in which one of the most prominent citizens is a former topless dancer. Prominent citizens aren't always business tycoons, politicians or socialites. On June 16, 1964—a date worth recording—Big Davey Rosenberg, the Condor publicist, asked Carol Doda, a Condor waitress, to dance in a topless swimsuit created by noted designer Rudi Gernreich. She did it, and San Francisco has never been the same since. Carol's act included her being lowered from the ceiling on a white grand piano. Soon the topless craze swept San Francisco and, in fact, the country. Bust enhancement kept Carol in the headlines. Later, she became the proprietor of a lingerie boutique on Union Street but she is still seen around North Beach where she is almost instantly recognized, as she should be.

———•·•———

A Topless Mother of Eight

Broadway: The Golden Years by Dick Boyd (El Cid)
PHOTO: ALAN CANTERBURY

A NORTH BEACH CLUB CALLED EL CID, now the New Sun Hong Kong Restaurant in the multi-story building covered with murals, at the northwest corner of Columbus and Broadway, was headquarters for the second topless dancer in North Beach. She was Gayle Spiegelman, billed as the "Topless Mother of Eight." Gayle opened in October of 1964. Actually she was my favorite. She really did have eight kids.

What did movie, sex kitten actress Jayne Mansfield and Gayle Spiegelman have in common besides an urge to display their chests for fun and profit? Both were decapitated in horrific auto accidents.

The Persian Kitten

YVONNE D'ANGIER, billed as the "Persian Kitten," danced in North beach at the Off-Broadway, on Kearny Street. She was an Iranian citizen and was later threatened with deportation on morals charges. Flamboyant attorney Melvin Belli intervened. Some say he married her to provide her with U.S. citizenship. Not a bad idea, but I can find no record of that.

A Topless Shoeshine Stand

I RECALL A TOPLESS SHOESHINE STAND at the southwest corner of Columbus and Broadway. It was sometime in the 1960s. There were also topless bands, a pool hall with topless pool players and a topless ice cream joint. Some clubs began featuring bottomless entertainers in 1967. I'm tempted to say, things went down from there.

Anyway, without puritanical bull bleep, the sexual revolution was in full swing then. The legal criteria for obscenity were being challenged by comic Lenny Bruce and others. What a great city, I thought. And I still think that, in spite of joints that frequently appeal to prurient rather than artistic interests—much of it from suburbanites and other tourists who apparently have never seen bare breasts where they come from. If a woman wants to take her shirt off and a man wants to ogle her, so be it.

"Shall We Have Brandy After Lunch?"

WE CONCLUDE OUR PANTHEON OF SAN FRANCISCO MADAMS with Marlene Brandy Baldwin, a resourceful creature, now retired in Northern California, and re-invented as the successful operator of an organization with a less problematic product. Brandy was the most well-known madam of the 1970s and 80s. For a madam, that can be both good and a bad. Good, because there was never a dearth of customers, bad, because the prominence led to frequent police busts. Brandy Baldwin's high profile, sporting life prompted the late *San Francisco Chronicle* columnist, Charles McCabe to write "She is a by-word in some of the more posh of the bars and restaurants of the financial district. When the meal is consumed, and the dice cups are put away, the frequent query, accompanied by the appropriate leer, is: 'Brandy after lunch?'"

On the negative side, in one highly-publicized "bust" Brandy either fell while trying to escape, or was pushed from a third floor window of her bagnio on Sacramento Street, and was severely injured. This did not stop her true calling however, and she continued to be in the police and public eye as a parlor house operator. She did some hard time and following one conviction was sentenced to 90 days in a nunnery. It's true.

To be sure there have been other madams and other parlor houses worthy of consideration in this galloping account of the San Francisco demimonde. From time to time we hear of what the newspapers now call "houses of ill-fame" surfacing here and there. But these discoveries are like the anxious birdwatcher's sighting of a rare woodpecker. There are no parlor houses in San Francisco today. Or, so we believe. But then again, entrepreneurial enterprise being what it is, who knows.

Enrico Banducci
PHOTO: PETER BREINIG, AUTHOR'S COLLECTION

Enrico Banducci and the hungry i

AS I HAVE SAID, San Franciscans have always welcomed those larger-than-life characters that for good, or occasionally ill, have colored the city's history. We are attuned to their celebrity. Indeed, we foster it and relish their presence or their memory. One such character who comes to mind and whose presence deserves attention, was the Italian-American Enrico Banducci, proprietor of the late and lamented hungry i, perhaps the most influential showroom in American cabaret history.

Enrico Banducci came to San Francisco from Bakersfield at fourteen, to pursue a career as a classical violinist. He brought with him the yellow-varnished violin he had been playing since he was five, and $10,000 he had saved from performing Mozart, Mendelssohn, Beethoven and Bach for service clubs in Kern County. His father, "an Italian bootlegger who made the best *grappa* in the area," said Banducci, made the boy practice in the garage and referred to his violin as "that squeaky box."

In San Francisco the enterprising youngster found a room in a boarding house at Jackson and Gough Streets and enrolled in Lowell High School. The boarding house was operated by Madame Bernet, second violinist for the San Francisco Symphony—$20 a month, room, breakfast and dinner, he recalled. Soon the young violinist from Bakersfield was playing concerts around town. "I was doing fairly well, but finally realized I was never going to be a major violinist so I decided to become an operatic baritone instead," he said.

After graduating from Lowell, he studied voice and began singing around town. "I sang at the Bocce Ball in North Beach, places like that," he recalled. But restless, and deciding he would never have the discipline to become either a concert violinist or an operatic baritone, he began moving from job to job—first with a local company that operated a string of movie houses and later with a wine distributor. During World War II he was classified 4F because of congenital vision impairment and worked as an electrician in a nearby shipyard. He also married the daughter of the second violist for the symphony. It didn't last. After the war he moved to New York, knocked about for a while, and undertook to promote the career of actress Luba Sharoff, later to become his second of four wives. In 1948 he returned to San Francisco, took one job and then another and finally opened a restaurant. He called it Enrico's Fine Foods, and at that point adopted his trademark black beret. The restaurant lasted six months.

In 1949 Enrico Banducci met Eric "Big Daddy" Nord, a Rabelaisian free spirit who operated a local hangout, Club des Artistes, at 149 Columbus Avenue in North Beach. That meeting was to change the course of Banducci's life. Nord wanted out. Banducci wanted in. He bought the club for $800, and its name was changed to the hungry i.

Why the hungry i? he was asked interminably. "One day we were trying to come up with a new name for my club. Someone said (it wasn't me) 'how about the Hungry Intellect?' Bingo! The hungry i it was—all lowercase, just to establish that we weren't white bread."

The first thing the fledging club owner did was to establish an entertainment policy. His first booking was Stella Brooks, a jazz singer. Soon he was booking local guitarists, singers and other performers. Business was pretty good. A year later, feeling expansive, Banducci moved the hungry i to a large cellar close by on Jackson between Kearny and Columbus. The unwieldy subterranean space had a red brick wall at one end. "We put our small stage against this wall." Soon Banducci was booking unknown comics and folk singers, and standing them up against that red brick wall, which became a much copied, hungry i trademark.

An early comic booked by Banducci was Mort Sahl who wound up appearing in the theater-club four years. He quoted Sahl as saying "Enrico saved me from selling cars in Southern California."

Banducci told me: We were beginning to attract a lot of college kids from around the Bay Area. I told Mort he should take off his tie, wear a baggy sweater and carry a folded newspaper under his arm. That's what I thought college kids did. In the beginning I paid him $75 a week and for five weeks he did nothing. After a while his rapid-fire monologues caught on. His humor was topical. It came right off the front-page headlines. Things were looking up." At that point *Holiday Magazine* ran an article about San Francisco and used the hungry i as an example of fresh new things that were happening here. "We were in the right place at the right time." Soon comics, vocal groups and other acts trying to make their name, wanted to come to San Francisco and stand up in front of that old brick wall in North Beach.

Professor Irwin Corey, self-styled as "The World's Foremost Authority," was a great favorite at the club. Banducci recalled: "I found him in Europe doing Army shows. The first time I booked him he stayed twenty-nine weeks. He walked out on stage and stared at the audience without saying a word. He would just stare. Finally, after stretching that silence to the breaking point he would scream out 'However....'

"Around 1958 I went to Chicago to audition Shelley Berman. He was playing at an improv club on a bill with Mike Nichols and Elaine May. Shelley was eager to play the hungry i and I booked him for $350 a week for six weeks. When Mike Nichols heard this he came up to me and said 'Now what are we going to do? You're taking our star away.' I sent Mike and Elaine to a friend in New York who had a small club and they were a hit. Then later I booked them at $500 a week for each. Like Mort Sahl they scored big with the college crowd out here. The audience could relate to their slice-of-life, improvised dialogue."

Lenny Bruce, who was described as a "verbal Hieronymus Bosch" by the late music critic and social commentator Ralph J. Gleason, headlined at the hungry i well before his highly documented obscenity arrests and subsequent court battles. "Lenny was a particular favorite of mine. Sometimes when he dropped a zinger, some in the audience would storm out and demand their money back. I gave it to them. We had a $5 per person door charge in those days," he said.

Banducci was one of the first to headline African American comics. "Dick Gregory had been doing church socials. I got Godfrey Cambridge early in his career. Richard Pryor was always hanging around wanting a chance so I finally put him on. I got Bill Cosby from Philadelphia for $400 a week. He was an unknown out here. He stayed the club twenty-six weeks the first time I booked him."

Banducci continued: "I saw Jonathan Winters on the Steve Allen TV Show. He was just a struggling comic at that point. He was funny, like in the word *peculiar*. I booked him at $800 a week. He did one bit where he talked to his mythical St. Bernard. 'Now Rufus, what did I tell you, you're not supposed to drink the brandy and eat the people. You're supposed to give them the brandy and save their lives.'

"Phyllis Diller came to me: 'I'm funny, put me on,' she said. At that time I owned half of the Purple Onion around the corner on Columbus so I put her in there and she talked about her relationship with her husband. She called him Fang. She was a very funny lady. Later she played the hungry i and was a smash.

"I had Barbra Streisand and Woody Allen on the same bill at $350 a week for each. In the beginning they died out there. No one knew them and no one cared. That was 1962. She was nineteen. Woody was still in his twenties. When he walked out on stage, total silence, but he could make me laugh. After four or five weeks with very little business, they both began to build an audience.

Pushed as to how he had happened to book Streisand, Banducci said "I was in New York looking for acts and I visited the booking agent Irving Arthur. We were in his office talking and the door was open. Suddenly I heard someone yelling from the outer office. 'Is that that guy Banducci from the coast? He should book me. I'm going to be famous.' Irving yelled back at her: 'Barbra get out of here. I'm trying to sell Banducci some talent.' I decided to take a chance on her although I hadn't heard her sing."

Over the twenty years the hungry i operated, Banducci also presented Tom Lehrer, Bob Newhart, Carmen McRae, Josh White, Carol Sloane, Miriam Makeba, Maya Angelou, the Kingston Trio, the

Limeliters (Banducci chose the name for the then-unknown trio), and Peter, Paul and Mary.

Riding high with the hungry i, the flamboyant Banducci opened Enrico's, a North Beach coffeehouse on Broadway, in 1958. Even if he had never operated the hungry i, the establishment of Enrico's would earn him a place in that pantheon of those remembered for contributing to the quality of life in this city. Enrico had wanted to open a European style coffeehouse that served food outdoors. State officials refused him the necessary permit. It wasn't sanitary to dine outdoors by the sidewalk, he was told. Determined, he collected snapshots of then highly popular drive-ins and requested another hearing on the subject. His pitch was that if they turned him down on the coffeehouse, they would have to close every drive-in up and down the state of California. "Why was it okay to eat in a parking lot and not in a sidewalk café?" he asked. He got his permit.

Enrico's became an overnight success. Socialites, politicians, columnists, cops, local hipsters, out-on-the-town, out-of-towners and assorted night people—all flocked to Enrico's. It was the place to hang out for a few more hours when Broadway began to shut down for the night. If you were lucky, local newspaper columnist Herb Caen might be there and the next day you could read about who else had been there and who said what. Banducci strolled between the tables playing his violin. Sometimes he burst into song. He was a legend in his own time. He went into the kitchen and cooked pasta for Dorothy Malone, Frank Sinatra, Peter Lawford, Burgess Meredith, Paul Newman and his wife Joanne Woodward and other celebrities who were turning up. He lived in a penthouse apartment on nearby Telegraph Hill. He owned a 55-foot sailing ketch and an airplane. On weekends he flew up to his 1,000-acre ranch in Northern California where he kept a string of horses. Enrico Banducci was quoted in the dailies and in national magazines. The hungry i, where so many careers had been launched, had made him a celebrity.

In 1962 he opened another venture, Clown Alley, the quintessential hamburger joint, on Columbus, a short block from the old hungry i.

"I needed a place to get a good hamburger," he said, and recalled that Barbra Streisand helped him open it by serving burgers and fries. Later, he sold it to his accountant.

Enrico's is still operating. He long ago sold the name and has no interest in it. He never sold the name, hungry i.

Sadly, the hungry i closed in 1970. The old International Hotel at Kearny and Jackson Streets (the hungry i was in the basement of the hotel building) was to be razed. Banducci lost his lease. He tried for a time to revive the "eye" as it was called by insiders, and in 1971 re-opened it in nearby Ghirardelli Square. But it was not to be. It closed within a year.

At that point Enrico dropped out. He moved to Richmond, Virginia where his son Gregory lived at the time, and opened a hotdog stand. Then, a few years ago, he returned. "I missed San Francisco. I feel better here," he said.

As suggested earlier, Banducci was one of those larger-than-life characters whose presence has added color and panache to the kooky charm that feeds the San Francisco myth. His hungry i contributed to the city's sophistication and artistic reputation.

What is Banducci's legacy? I once asked him what he thought that might be: He thought about it for a moment and then said "Well, the hungry i was in the right place at the right time. I tried to book acts that appealed to me. I believe that had some lasting effect."

The Saloon Piano Player

Don Asher and his long-time companion Dr. Lois Goodwill
PHOTO: FROM THE COLLECTION OF DR. LOIS GOODWILL

THE OTHER DAY I CLEANED OUT A CLOSET and found a March 1970 *Holiday Magazine*, then a big, glossy publication read by big, glossy, discerning travelers with lots of discretionary income. The March 1970 issue, which I saved all these years, devoted a 120-page special issue to San Francisco, "The city of Infinite Possibilities." Tucked into those pages was a piece called "Culture and Counterculture."

A full page, color photo of a group of serious and determined San Franciscans at the Minimum Daily Requirement—a North Beach coffeehouse—accompanied the article. It was captioned: "The literati gather at the MDR." Right in the center of the portrait was a small man in a blue work shirt identified only as Don Asher. He was surrounded by a group of heavy-hitting, high profile, local writers: Jessica Mitford, Paul Jacobs, Evan Connell Jr., Don Carpenter, Barnaby Conrad and Herbert Gold. Gold had written the *Holiday* article. Don Asher stared out of the photo of that powerhouse circle displaying both confidence and modesty.

He's been gone now since 2010. Seeing his image in the old *Holiday Magazine* got me reflecting on saloon pianists, a wonderful subspecies of professional musicians. They bring a high degree of class to our saloons—a few standards from the Great American songbook, some blues, a little Harlem stride and maybe even a bit of lock-hand boogie woogie like Meade "Lux" Lewis's "Honky Tonk Train." That's the essence of saloon piano. It's like having a pianist playing your favorite tunes in your living room. So here is the quintessential saloon piano player Don Asher, and a few comments on some of his keyboard compatriots.

Don Asher came to San Francisco in 1959 from his hometown Worchester, Massachusetts and discovered that the city did have "infinite possibilities." He became house piano player for Enrico Banducci's groundbreaking nightclub-theater the hungry i.

*

"I used to go almost every night to the hungry i to catch Don Asher, the pianist. Or Mort Sahl or Woody Allen when he was just starting."—Barnaby Conrad, author, artist and nightclub operator, in his book Name Dropping.

*

"I needed a piano player to back up the acts. It was as simple as that. Asher was a nice quiet man. He said what he had to say with the piano and also with words on the printed page."—Enrico Banducci, dean of the talent spotters who brought nineteen-year-old Barbra Streisand and many other soon-to-be famous stars to the hungry i.

*

"I had no idea he was a writer. I thought of him only as a piano player. He asked me to read some of his short stories. They were good. I told him to tell the story of his life as a piano player and make it funny. He did. He wrote a memoir

called Notes from a Battered Grand, *and a fine, semi-autobiographical novel,* Piano Sport."—*Herbert Gold, prolific San Francisco writer of award-winning novels and non-fiction.*

*

Many years ago I interviewed Don Asher for a magazine piece. This is what he told me:

"I am the product of a nice middle class Jewish family from Worchester (he pronounced it "Woosta."). My mother pushed me and I took lessons from a classical piano instructor—one dollar for a half hour lesson. I did well with my scales and arpeggios but something else was in the air, or rather the air waves—Benny Goodman, Artie Shaw, Count Basie, just to name a few giants. That was when there was two-a-day vaudeville in movie houses and I heard Charlie Barnet and the Tommy Dorsey and Jimmy Dorsey bands. And 40 miles away in Boston was the Hi-Hat Club, and playing there was the piano god of us all, Art Tatum. Like many other kids at the time I made an exciting passage from classical piano to jazz.

"Right in my hometown I met a piano playing demon named Jaki Bayard, who later became a jazz legend. He was the fire by which all of us warmed our hands. So I dropped my one dollar classical piano teacher and gave Jaki fifty cents a lesson. I got good enough to play in dives, gin mills and stripper joints. Then it was on to resorts and dancehalls along the Boston Turnpike.

"One day something stopped me cold in *Time Magazine.* It was a photo of a buddy from Cornell, which I had attended. The photo showed Kenneth Rexroth reciting his poetry to a jazz accompaniment in a San Francisco club called The Cellar. And there was my buddy from Cornell playing tenor sax behind Rexroth. This was in 1958, near the end of the Beat era. At that moment I decided San Francisco was where I wanted to be, so I moved west.

"In North Beach I ran into Faith Winthrop, a girl singer I knew from Cape Cod. She was singing at the hungry i. She needed a piano accompanist. I got the job. After the last set Enrico Banducci took me aside and said 'When can you start steady?' Suddenly I was house pianist at the hungry i. I played the acts on and off stage, accompanied them, or played soft background music during their routines.

"For some reason comics always think the piano player is funny. Frequently they direct parts of their routines at piano players, actually including us in their acts. Jack E. Leonard thought it was open season on piano players.

'What key are you in sonny boy?'

'D-flat.'

'And you certainly are.'

"One night after playing introductions for Mort Sahl I slid off the piano bench and headed for the bar. Sahl's voice knifed over the speakers.

'Mister Asher, have you ever contemplated another means of livelihood?'

"No, have you?" I replied. It got a big laugh.

"But I'm not a comic; I'm a saloon piano player. You have to be fast with your fingers and be able to improvise. Once, a very good piano player, Jess Stacey, said 'I don't look for every note to be a pearl. Sometimes they turn out to be meatballs. If you sense a meatball, a clinker, or a clam coming on, you have only a few seconds at most to figure out how you are going to use it to your musical advantage.'"

I am indebted to Mary Etta Moose, one of the treasures of North Beach, for helping me recall the glory days of the saloon piano players, many of whom I had forgotten.

Ed and Mary Etta Moose and their business partner Sam Deitsch brought many top saloon pianists to their much-missed Washington Square Bar & Grill, and later across the park to Moose's. I was around for those glory years.

There was a Sunday afternoon when Norma Teagarden, sister of the legendary jazz trombonist Jack Teagarden, played at "The Square" (as we regulars called it). Norma and her mother Helen played four-handed piano. Jack played his trombone and his brother Charlie blew trumpet licks.

Mike Lipskin, stride piano man—now an entertainment lawyer—had an intellectual exercise when he played "The Square's" old upright. He propped a copy of the *Wall Street Journal* on the music stand and affected reading it while he played. I was suckered into believe him.

And you might remember Dick Vartanian, the saloon piano player who wore a turban when he played at the old Rickshaw Bar in Chinatown's Ross Alley. I thought I owned the Rickshaw. I hung out there so much. Whenever I walked in and Vartanian spied me from the piano bar, he stopped playing whatever tune he was into and began a slow, sexy version of Teach Me Tonight—my favorite show-tune to this day.

But digressions are creeping into this back story and there's no room to expound on other saloon pianists who frequently made my day—and my nights. Other artists like Lou Levy who played for his partner-vocalist Pinky Winters, Burt Bales, Mike Greensil, Jeannie Hoffman, Gini Wilson, John Horton Cooper, and the incomparable Earl 'Fatha' Hines. I'm sure there are other giants that I have forgotten. My memory needs refreshing.

————•◦•————

Ron Boise and the Kama Sutra

YOU DON'T HEAR MUCH ABOUT RON BOISE and his scrap metal, junkyard sculpture anymore. Yet, at one time in North Beach, this brilliant artist was the center of a legal maelstrom that posed the question: Is it art or is it obscenity? It was art, and although it graphically depicted sexual love in its many variations, it was clearly not obscene.

Ron Boise was born in Colorado in 1932 and died in Texas of a liver ailment in 1966. He was the creator of an incredible series of small, welded-metal statues based on the *Kama Sutra*, the classic Indian text on lovemaking. Boise was a prominent figure in North Beach in the late 1950s and early 60s, and a friend of novelist Ken Kesey and his Merry Pranksters.

Here's an update on the Ron Boise story along with a personal sidebar.

In 1964 Boise's *Kama Sutra* sculptures were being exhibited in the Vorpal Gallery, at that time in the North Beach alley between City Lights and Vesuvio's bar. Now it's called Jack Kerouac Alley. One day the San Francisco police arrived at the gallery and confiscated the Boise statues for being obscene. Vorpal Gallery owner, Muldoon Elder, was arrested for displaying Boise's sculptures. There would be a jury trial.

Just before the trial John Bryan, a local counterculture figure of the day, published a magazine called *Notes from Underground*. He ran a black-and-white photo of one of the Boise Kama Sutra pieces on the cover and others in a big spread inside. In an accompanying article Bryan said "The disturbing thing is that such an arrest could occur here long after the community has made it clear that we have no room in this town for anymore witch hunts in the arts." Just a few

Sculpture by Ron Boise from author's collection
PHOTO: ERNEST BEYL

years earlier, in 1961, Lenny Bruce, another kind of artist, was busted for obscenity at the Jazz Workshop on Broadway. In that 1962 trial Bruce was acquitted.

Also accompanying the photos of the *Kama Sutra* statues in *Notes from Underground*, Alan Watts, the Zen philosopher, was quoted from a talk he gave in a Big Sur gallery, when Boise's *Kama Sutra* pieces were exhibited there a year earlier without a bust. Watts said at that time "Here is a sculptor who is doing something which I call 'pushing the line back'—in the same way as great modern writers such as Henry Miller, D.H. Lawrence and James Joyce have been pushing the line back in literature." Watts went on to say that instead of getting away with murder, Boise was "...getting away with love." A nice way to put it.

The Ron Boise *Kama Sutra* case went to court and Muldoon Elder was acquitted.

I first met Ron Boise in the 1960s, before the big Vorpal Gallery bust. He had moved to funky Venice in Southern California. I ran into him there in a coffeehouse-crash pad called The Gas House. It was operated by entrepreneurial party pad operator Eric "Big Daddy" Nord, who, with some encouragement from San Francisco authorities, left North Beach for what, to him, was the more tolerant and salubrious Venice. Nord introduced me to Boise and we had a few mugs of red wine together and talked about life, love and his work. At one point he said he was in need of some cash and asked if I would like to purchase one of his sculptures. I had a few bucks at the time and agreed to go to his nearby studio above an out-of-business grocery store. There, in the center of a large loft, was a pile of rusted, auto body parts and the tools of his art—metal cutters, wooden mallets, and welding equipment. There were also dozens of completed junk metal sculptures. All were human figures either alone or entwined with others. I picked one out and Boise sold it to me for $75. I still have the piece and am looking at it now as I write this. My Ron Boise sculpture is of a standing male figure about two-and-a-half feet tall, head turned aside, legs apart and one arm over his chest; the other thrust back in a dismissive manner. There is an attached female figure crouched at his feet. She has both arms wrapped around his calf, her cheek pressed to his thigh. It's a powerful work suggesting some inner sexual turmoil.

Several years later I was passing the Vorpal Gallery which had by then moved below Telegraph Hill to Battery Street between Union and Filbert. I glanced in and recognized the work of Ron Boise. Some were life sized; others quite small. Obviously I had to enter. A young woman came over to me to offer assistance and I told her that I admired Ron Boise's work and had one of his pieces. "I wonder what it's worth?" I said, and asked if Muldoon Elder, the gallery owner, was there. She excused herself and went through a door, presumably into Muldoon's office. A few minutes later she returned and said "Muldoon is busy right now but he says you can't have a Ron Boise sculpture because he knows where they all are."

"Well, he doesn't know where this one is," I said and blustered out of the gallery.

I chaffed over the incident for a couple of days. Then one afternoon I took a Polaroid photo of my Boise statue and walked down to the Vorpal Gallery. Inside was the same young woman. I showed her the photo and asked her to show it to Muldoon. I thought Muldoon would come shooting out of his office but he didn't. The young woman came back, handed me my Polaroid and said "Muldoon is on a long distance call and will be out in a few minutes but he told me to ask you how much you want for it."

"It's not for sale," I said and left. And that's how I almost got to meet Muldoon Elder back then. The Vorpal Gallery closed a few years ago and I always wondered what kind of a guy Muldoon was. So one day I went over to his apartment to finally meet him. He's a great storyteller and we had a good laugh over the Vorpal Gallery story.

These days, Muldoon Elder is painting, writing poetry, short stories and fables after the fashion of the Greek slave Aesop.

I still have my Ron Boise statue and it's still not for sale.

———•◦•———

The Automatic Human Jukebox

Grimes Poznikov, the Automatic Human Jukebox
PHOTO: COURTESY OF CINDY RUSSELL / FLICKR.COM: CINDYR

AN INTERESTING WRINKLE ON COMEDY in San Francisco is provided by Street Performers—jugglers, fire-eaters, mimes, comic singers and others. Certainly one of the most unusual of these was the Automatic Human Jukebox, Grimes Poznikov. There probably won't be another like him on the streets of San Francisco.

Poznikov has my vote as the most comic of the San Francisco Street performers. A shadowy figure hidden inside a cardboard refrigerator packing case, Poznikov, the Automatic Human Jukebox, remained silent inside his packing case until a passerby inserted a dollar bill into a slot in the cardboard. The bill immediately disappeared, pulled mysteriously within the dark interior of the apparatus. The "player" of the jukebox then selected a tune by pushing the appropriate small, painted circle on the face of the box. At that point, a cardboard flap flipped up and a battered trumpet poked out in attack mode. Then came a bleating rendition of "April in Paris" or whatever. That was Poznoikov's gig.

Back then, he was an unseen but prominent street performer who hung out at The Cannery, along with others who strutted their stuff for the crowds of tourists and locals who still gather there. Pitched somewhere between comedy and tragedy, Poznikov was Man inexorably reduced to Machine.

Just where he fits into a long history of San Francisco comics and comedy could be the subject for scholarly debate, but he certainly was funny in a Chaplinesque manner.

Grimes Poznokov died a few years ago after becoming homeless and living beneath a highway overpass.

———•◦•———

Robin Williams
and the Human Game Preserve

"SAN FRANCISCO IS A HUMAN GAME PRESERVE," said comedian-actor Robin Williams who lived in the San Francisco Bay Area and was adopted by locals with a finely-tuned sense of humor. An improvisational master, Williams was driven and manic.

Robin Williams
PHOTO: DARSIE / WIKIMEDIA COMMONS

Although born in Chicago, his parents moved to the San Francisco Bay Area when Williams was in his senior year in high school. He studied political science in Claremont Men's College, trained as an actor at Marin College and later at Juilliard in New York City. When he returned to California he performed stand-up comedy on the club circuit. His first real break came after an appearance at the Comedy Store in Los Angeles. He was soon appearing on TVs resurrection of "Laugh-In" and later in his own show, "Mork and Mindy." Dramatic movie performances in the *World According to Garp, Good Morning Vietnam, Good Will Hunting, Jakob the Liar* and *One Hour Photo,* turned him into a high-in-demand, bona fide movie star. But to many he was simply the fastest quip in the west.

PART FIVE

Through the Magic Lantern

THESE DAYS San Francisco's citizens—whether they are called "techies" or some other type of end-of-the-rainbow seekers—are not unlike those who followed their dreams westward in the early days. For every roughneck miner and adventurer, there were smart, creative, self-motivated, self-starters. Merchants like Levi Strauss who changed the way the world dresses. Businessmen like railroad barons Collis P. Huntington, Mark Hopkins, Leland Stanford and Charles Crocker. Bankers like A. P. Giannini who financed San Francisco after the 1906 Earthquake and Fire. Now, just as then, ambitious folks come here for the food and drink, the entertainment—The Good Life—and to get rich. Has San Francisco changed that much? I don't think so.

Joe DiMaggio, 1941
PHOTO: WIKIMEDIA COMMONS

Joltin Joe

A LONG TIME AGO—not in another galaxy but right here in North Beach—I was driving down Columbus Avenue with one of my sons, about twelve at the time. At a traffic signal I stopped and glanced in the rear view mirror.

"Mike," I said excitedly, "don't turn around now but Joe Di Maggio is driving the car behind us."

It was that moment that told me irrefutably that I was neglecting my father-son bonding. Not only was I failing in baseball, but probably in pop music and movies. Yes, he really did say "Dad, just who is Joe DiMaggio?"

Here in North Beach we enjoy naming places after famous Italians. Two that come to mind quickly are Caffe Puccini and Joe DiMaggio Playground. Hanging on the wall in Caffe Puccini are framed operatic scores in the composer's hand. Okay, so they're reproductions. Do you know any other place besides the Giacomo Puccini Archives in Milan where you can see stuff like this? Well, that's my segue to Joe DiMaggio Playground. DiMaggio died in 1999 at eighty-four and the Florida lawyer who controlled his estate didn't want to let us put up signs reading Joe DiMaggio Playground—even though Joltin' Joe played ball there as a North Beach kid. Back in 2000 San Francisco Mayor Willie Brown bit the bullet, and the signs were put up.

Operation Midnight Climax

IT'S NOT EXACTLY HOT NEWS that there were bordellos, brothels and bagnios in the early days of sprightly San Francisco. There were many houses of ill-fame, as they say, in the raunchy Gold Rush town's Latin Quarter (now North Beach) and on adjacent Telegraph Hill.

But not as well-known, is that a full-fledged fancy house existed on Telegraph Hill as late as the 1960s. But what about this? The Telegraph Hill bordello (it was in a bay view apartment on the north slope) was operated by the CIA and we're not talking here about the Culinary Institute of America.

The super spy agency operated the house to test unsanctioned, mind-altering drugs in a kind of *Manchurian Candidate,* brainwashing brainstorm, and the story has more unexpected twists than a Thelonius Monk piano solo.

Not one of the CIA's most inspired projects, the Bordello of Telegraph Hill came about like this: By 1953 the agency already had an active program searching for truth serum and behavior-controlling drugs that it hoped might lead to clandestine political assassinations and other such noble pursuits. In the midst of this mind-elevating activity, the agency happened upon lysergic acid diethylamide and became intent on exploring Ken Kesey-like, Merry Prankster, LSD acid dreams. It wanted to test this and other magic potions in real-life interrogation situations and to see if a person under their influence could be made to do bad things just like in the movies. First, it did its testing within the agency in boyish, *Animal House*-type pranks. Agents never knew when they were going to embark on a wacky trip after downing a little party punch. Later, the CIA opened a bordello in New York's Greenwich Village to test pharmaceutical LSD and other substances. Then, came the tragic death of a civilian biochemist working for the government who, without his knowing it, was given a huge dose of LSD at a CIA conference on biological warfare. Several days later, in a depression, he plunged to his death from a New York hotel room.

At that point the agency moved the bordello operation to a Telegraph Hill safe house, a sleek, three-story apartment building in a quiet neighborhood. It engaged a tough-talking, ex-undercover agent for the Federal Bureau of Narcotics named Dr. George Hunter White, who then hired and managed the prostitutes. Operation Midnight Climax was underway. The San Francisco hookers were paid to lure eager customers to the Telegraph Hill apartment and were served LSD-laced cocktails. The stylish, playboy "pad" on the Hill was tastefully decorated with French posters and was bugged with microphones in lighting fixtures that connected to out-of-sight tape recorders. Another CIA agent sat on a toilet seat behind a two-way mirror and observed. The "pad" was said to cost about $2,000 per month in rental fees and operated until 1965.

Much of this information was brought to light when it was unclassified under the Freedom of Information Act. Today, it can be found in political newsletters, various websites, on the pages of some prominent periodicals and even in one well-circulated book on the history of Telegraph Hill. The apartment that was the center for Operation Midnight Climax is still there looking out over San Francisco Bay.

———•◦•———

Finnochio's: What a Drag

Vintage Finnochio's night club promotional postcard featuring female impersonators
PHOTO: AUTHOR'S COLLECTION

FINNOCHIO'S, a saucy nightclub that featured female impersonators, was once a big attraction in North Beach.

Female impersonation has a long history in San Francisco. It began right after gold was discovered at Sutter's Mill in 1848. In 1850, the Jenny Lind Theater featured Shakespeare's Twelfth Night—a comedy in which a male actor, playing a woman, pretends to be a man.

Our city has nurtured a long list of female impersonators in this hilarious journey through the years. So here with a wild leap through time, let's land at Finnochio's.

Joe Finnochio, an Italian immigrant, worked in his father's North Beach speakeasy. One night a customer who had tasted a little too much of the "sauce" provided by the establishment, performed a shaky but moving performance mimicking the legendary vaudeville singer Sophie Tucker who was billed frequently as "The Last of the Red Hot Mamas." This gave Joe Finnochio an idea for Red Hot Mamas in drag that would continue to excite San Francisco for more than sixty years.

And, by the way, the word "finnochio"—and that was Joe's real family name—is the Italian word for fennel, the licorice-scented bulb used frequently to flavor Italian cookery. A less salubrious and now antiquated definition of "finnochio" is what most of us now call "gay."

Joe Finnochio opened his own speakeasy in 1929 at 406 Stockton Street. He featured a female impersonator as part of a floor show. It was a modest beginning. When prohibition was repealed in 1933 he expanded it, and then in 1936, exuberant with his success, moved to a North Beach location. There he began featuring elaborate productions with lots of pizzazz and glittery costumes. Despite San Francisco's tradition of risqué entertainment, there was a police bust shortly after the Broadway opening. Joe Finnochio was arrested for "keeping a disorderly house and selling liquor after 2 a.m." Apparently the issue of the entertainers mingling with the customers was a no-no.

Joe promised to run his club in an orderly fashion—like a theater, he said. And down through the years he did, with scores of female impersonators appearing on his stage. Some became well-known personalities. Among Finnochio's headliners was Lucien Phelps, a Sophie Tucker expert who starred for twenty-seven years. Another was Don McLean, whose stage name was Lori Shannon. He became known nationally after playing the Archie Bunker drag queen on TV's "All in the Family." He had a great opening line to his Finnochio's act: "Welcome to Boy's Town. I'm Father Flanagan."

Not only did locals flock to Finnochio's but visiting celebrities did as well. Bob Hope, Frank Sinatra, Bette Davis and Tallulah Bankhead (the real ones), all made the scene. Howard Hughes escorted Ava Gardner to Finnochio's. There was a rumor in 1945 that Errol Flynn and David Niven had escorted one of the Finnochio's stars (Pussy Kat) to a suite at the Fairmont Hotel. Hollywood gossip columnist Louella Parsons got wind of it but her publisher forbade her to run the story.

Joe Finnochio died in 1986 at eighty-eight years. His wife Eve kept Finnochio's alive until 1999. Citing a rent increase and dwindling attendance, she finally closed it, packed up the props, swept up the glitter and retired to live with her memories.

Female impersonation had reached the mainstream. One no longer had to seek it out on Broadway.

When poet Lawrence Ferlinghetti heard the news that Finnochio's had closed he responded "What a drag."

Male Actress Charles Pierce

ANOTHER COMEDIAN San Francisco embraced enthusiastically was Charles Pierce whom columnist Herb Caen dubbed a "male actress." Pierce trained as an actor in the well-regarded Pasadena Playhouse and later was seen in several New York, off-Broadway shows. In the early 1950s he was doing comedy sketches and impersonations all over the country. But Pierce loved San Francisco and San Francisco loved him. Soon he was playing Ann's 440 Club in North Beach. By this time, billed as "The Master or Mistress of Surprise or Disguise," he was in drag. In time his routines included Bette Davis, Tallulah Bankhead, Marlene Dietrich, Katharine Hepburn, Joan Crawford, Carol Channing and Jeanette MacDonald. Other San Francisco clubs he played were the Gilded Cage, Bimbo's 365 Club, the Plush Room and even the grand Venetian Room at the Fairmont Hotel. Pierce died in 1999. No one has been able to fill his high heels.

Carol Channing spoke at his funeral in North Hollywood and said "He did Carol Channing better than I did."

Sweet Pam and the Cockettes

A FEW YEARS AGO a book was published about the Cockettes and I went right out to a local bookstore to pick it up. I didn't know in what section it might be in so asked the clerk.

"A book on what?" He asked.

"The Cockettes."

"Do you mean the Rockettes?"

"Well, not exactly, but something like that."

The clerk found the book on the computer—*Midnight at the Palace* by Pam Tent. It was in stock and I bought it and spent a long evening reading and reminiscing.

Now, if I had engaged in that bookstore conversation thirty years ago when the gender-bending, hippie, acid drag queens the Cockettes were playing the Palace Theater in North Beach, there would have been instant recognition. Liberal North Beach has always had room for those in the vanguard and tried to avoid the commonplace and the banal.

The Cockettes flamed at a high burn in San Francisco in 1969. By 1972 the flame had gone out. The group performed at midnight musical extravaganzas at the Palace, a long gone, 1300-seat movie theater on Powell Street Just off Columbus Avenue. It had a 1930s interior—a mélange of Chinese kitsch and art deco. There, in the waning—frequently ugly—days of psychedelic San Francisco, a strange bead-bedecked, tie-dyed crowd of Cockette worshippers, mingled with San Francisco socialites to cheer the outrageous performances. Audiences were shocked and thrilled at the same time. In the ornate Palace the smell of patchouli oil (the hippie Chanel No. 5) wafted to the ceiling along with the fashionable smell of sweet smoke. In the hours before midnight off-beat films were screened: episodes from Saturday

Sweet Pam, Scrumbly Koldewyn, Pristine Condition, Billy Orchid, Reggie and Tim (seated), 1972
PHOTO: COURTESY OF THE ESTATE OF CLAY GEERDES

matinee serials like Flash Gordon and Tarzan, Rudolph Valentino's Son of the Sheik and experimental underground movies.

Then at midnight, the Cockettes—more than a dozen gay, hippie men, a small group of women and even a few straight guys—who were addicted to Hollywood glamour and just liked to dress up—took to the stage. Their frequent below-the-waist nudity was not a costume malfunction. The Cockettes were a San Francisco sensation: louche, lewd, loopy, la di da. It is important to understand that the gay Cockettes were not female impersonators or transvestites. Many wore full beards along with their pasties and net stockings. There was a kind of masculine gayness about these queens. They weren't trying to fool anyone into thinking they were women. And they were uncommonly aggressive and in-your-face.

For those who missed those "Nocturnal Dream Shows," as they were billed, here are some eyebrow-raising titles of individual productions mounted by the Cockettes: Gone with the Showboat (to Oklahoma), Tinsel Tarts in a Hot Coma, The Fairy Tale Extravaganza, Tropical Heat Wave, Hollywood Babylon, Hell's Harlots, Les Cockettes Folies de Paris, Pearls Over Shanghai and Hot Greeks.

There were other astonishing performing arts groups elsewhere at about the same time: New York's Theater of the Ridiculous and the Living Theater, a nomadic troupe whose pacifist-anarchist political theater frequently ended in arrests, a group in Seattle called the Whiz Kidz, and Frank Zappa who was scandalizing Southern California. While these groups were far-out (to use the hippie vernacular of the time) they were basically structured on rock 'n' roll. The Cockettes were unique: offensive, indecent, deplorable or brilliant—take your pick. They knew no limits.

Pam Tent, who wrote Midnight at the Palace, subtitled "My Life as a Fabulous Cockette," was one of the few women in the group. She was known as Sweet Pam then. A shy youngster from Detroit, she came to San Francisco in the mid-sixties, wandered away for a while but always came back. One day just having returned to the Haight-Ashbury, she was sitting on a cardboard suitcase with her teddy bear. She had a sign hanging round her neck that read "Take Me Home." And that's just what happened. Hippie Marshall Olds took her home where she began living with him and his wife. Marshall and Sweet Pam later became Cockettes.

A dazzling charismatic figure who called himself Hibiscus (George Harris Jr.) was founder and the spiritual father of the Cockettes. He was a member of a prominent East Coast family of performers—musicians, dancers and songwriters. Later, when the Cockettes failed to live up to his idealistic concept and true hippie ethos, Hibiscus left and formed another troupe called Angels of Light.

Soon Sweet Pam was living in a communal hippie pad in a Victorian house. The group called itself Kaliflower, tried to follow the teachings of Karl Marx and was patterned after the precepts of the 19th Century, upstate New York, Oneida Commune, a utopian collective.

Some of Sweet Pam's Cockette companions were Scrumbly, Tahara, Jilala, Kreemah Ritz, Goldie Glitters, Harlow, Fayette, Divine and the legendary Hibiscus.

One midnight at the Palace in 1971, when the Cockettes were at the top of their popularity, Truman Capote and New York journalist Rex Reed showed up. Capote was uncharacteristically almost speechless, but he did manage to utter "This is the most outrageous thing I have ever seen."

Enthralled by the Cockettes, when Reed returned to New York he wrote glowingly in a widely syndicated column of what he had seen in San Francisco. Soon, a New York engagement for the dazzling hippie dragsters was planned.

In November 1971 they opened in New York at the Anderson Theater in the East Village with a loose rendition of "Tinsel Tarts." Everyone who was anyone (as they say) was there. John Lennon was in the audience; so was Gore Vidal. The Cockettes bombed! One newspaper headline read "Having no Talent is not Enough."—a Gore Vidal line.

When I once had a long conversation with Sweet Pam, her analysis of the New York debacle was: "They didn't know what we were all about. They expected something we were not. We were not a professional theatrical troupe. We were San Francisco hippies have a good time."

The show ran about a month and later played to good houses and the Cockettes were appreciated. Bob Dylan and New York's Mayor John Lindsay turned up. But the devastating reviews had done their damage.

Sweet Pam continued: "When we returned to San Francisco we went on for a while but we were splintering. We had already lost several Cockettes who had an itch to do their own solo acts.

"We finally broke up," said Sweet Pam. "One faction wanted to formalize the shows; make them more professional. Charge more for them. Another faction wanted to keep a high degree of spontaneity and informality; to offer our shows for free."

Today the Cockettes are only a memory. For a social scientist they were a treasure trove of the bazaar; a flash of drug-induced creativity that mixed sexual confusion with radical politics.

Underground movie maker John Waters who worked with the Cockettes on several films described what was taking place within the confines of the group: "sexual anarchy."

Fayette, another of the few women Cockettes, put it simply "People lived at the end of their imaginations."

And Sweet Pam commented: "People (the Cockettes) seldom said no to anything."

Where are they now? Several died of drug overdoses or of AIDS. Some are still with us. Last time I checked, Sweet Pam was an accountant in San Francisco and lived in the Oakland Hills She admitted to being half in and half out of the mainstream. In 1971 she married a fellow Cockette, Scrumbly, in a much publicized wedding on Marin County's Mt. Tamalpais. They later parted but the couple had a son. I brelieve he is now a Bay Area musician.

At the time I interviewed Sweet Pam, several of the survivors were still hanging out together and "re-expressing" themselves, as she described it. In scheduled salons they displayed photos, put on multimedia shows and even did some performances, tamed down by the standards of the old Cockettes. "We don't take our clothes off now," said Sweet Pam.

Besides the Pam Tent memoir, a highly-regarded 2002 film documentary on the Cockettes shown at the Sundance Film Festival provided a nostalgic overview.

Could the Cockettes phenomenon return? Not likely. Sweet Pam again: "Today being gay is so main stream. In those days every day was like a coming out party. Everyone was free to explore their own persona. We were bursting forth. Being gay seems different now. I think today it's more about gyms and bodybuilding. With us it wasn't so much about being gay. It was more about being whatever you wanted to be and to go wherever your imagination led you. We came out of the hippie movement and the whole thing exploded."

So what is the legacy of the Cockettes? Well, that depends on your take on pop culture. The Cockettes' kinky influence still pervades in the glitter rock scene. Consider David Bowie, Elton John, Cyndi Lauper, Alice Cooper, Marilyn Manson and campy Bette Midler.

Personally, I miss them. Certainly their lives were out of control. They crashed and burned. But for a brief period they had enormous energy, enthusiasm and they didn't give a damn about shop-worn conventions. They were free-spirited and independent. Isn't that the way proud parents like to describe their children?

Saxlady and the Mortuary Marching Band

Green Street Mortuary Marching Band
PHOTO: PETER BREINIG, AUTHORS COLLECTION

SAN FRANCISCO'S TOURISM GURUS may not realize it, but the Green Street Mortuary Marching Band here in North Beach ranks right up there with the most colorful attractions in the city. It is certainly one of the strangest—a profoundly religious and symbolic piece of street theater.

The band's brisk marches along the streets of North Beach and Chinatown at the head of an Asian funeral cortege, not only stop traffic but turn the heads of locals and tourists alike. The effect is awesome, a dramatic epiphany, evocative of the mysterious passage to the next world.

The Green Street Mortuary Marching Band is led by a blond dynamo, known as Saxlady who once played on the road with Duke Ellington and his band and later led the house band at North Beach's Finnochio's. Annually, Saxlady's marching band sends more than 300 Chinese and other Asians off to join their ancestors.

Playing western hymns like "Amazing Grace," "Onward Christian Soldiers" and "Nearer My God to Thee," the funeral marches are punctuated with muffled thumps of the bass drum, the snap and roll of a snare and the intermittent, almost random, banging of a Chinese gong.

A black, top-down convertible mounted with a life-sized color photo of the deceased, follows the ten-piece band. Next comes the hearse, then a number of closed limos and cars with family members and friends. Frequently the Christian, hymn-playing marching band is joined by a Buddhist ensemble in saffron robes, that burns incense and scatters spirit money to confuse bad spirits who may wish to unsettle the departed on that final journey.

The tradition of public mourning with musical accompaniment goes back centuries and has been practiced by many cultures. In New Orleans, for example, colorful marching bands play dirges as they escort the departed to the cemetery, and lively jazz tunes on the return. In China, Confucian worship and respect for ancestors began borrowing from western traditions. In the old British colonies, Hong Kong for example, colonial military officers and business leaders were ushered into the next world by marching brass bands. So it was a short step for prominent Chinese immigrants in turn-of-the-century San Francisco to be marched off to their destiny. The earliest traceable example was the 1892 funeral of "Little Pete," a rogue Chinese entrepreneur and gangster shot to death in a Washington Street barbershop.

The original Chinese funeral band was the Cathay Boys Club Band that played for important Chinese funerals. The practice continued for many years but gradually died out in the sixties.

Founded in 1909, the Green Street Mortuary, at 649 Green Street, opposite O'Reilly's Irish Pub and down the street from Fugazi Hall, revived the custom in the early nineties. Enter the Saxlady, Lisa Pollard, and well-known jazz trumpet man, John Coppola who played with Woody Herman and Stan Kenton at various times. Today band members are professional musicians and members of Local Six of the American Federation of Musicians. In 1992, the Green Street Mortuary, which handled many of the Italian-American funerals in North Beach, found it was also acquiring a sizable Chinese-American clientele. In a burst of civic interest it contacted Saxlady and the present band, complete with black uniforms topped by white nautical caps with gold trim, is the result. Today, many prominent citizens can't leave these worldly cares without it.

The half-hour march usually ends on the edge of North Beach. The Chinese gong sounds three times in final salute to the deceased and the band disperses—usually reconvening for a beer at a nearby joint. The funeral cortege is escorted out of town by uniformed, motorcycle rent-a-cops, to the cemetery in nearby Colma for burial.

While other cities with large Chinese-American communities have on occasion organized funeral bands on a one-off basis, the custom has largely died out. But here in San Francisco it has become a colorful and meaningful fixture keeping this cultural high-note alive.

Grace's Gardens

Grace Marchant in her garden, 1970s
PHOTO: COURTESY LARRY HABEGGER

ALTHOUGH I LIVED IN SAN FRANCISCO FROM DIAPERS, through short pants when my family lived way out on Turk Street in the sand dunes, it wasn't until adulthood and blue jeans that I moved to Telegraph Hill to be cool—and I mean cool in the vernacular sense of the word. Grace Marchant assisted me to develop my self-declared coolness. Grace lived on the Filbert Steps—half way between Montgomery and Sansome streets—right where Napier Lane, with its ancient wooden walkway, crosses it. One day looking for a San Francisco apartment, I ran into a high school girlfriend who lived in a tiny place on the Greenwich Steps. She took me up there and I was bitten—make that smitten. Anyway, she took me over to the Filbert Steps to meet Grace who was the queen of the hill. It was my lucky day. A week later, Grace found an apartment for me on the Greenwich Steps—sixty or more wooden steps up to Montgomery and sixty or more steps down to Sansome. Speedy's at Union and Montgomery delivered the groceries.

Grace Marchant was the constant gardener. Her legacy, the Grace Marchant Gardens, was carved out of the steep, eastern slope of Telegraph Hill on each side of the steps. Grace, who had been a Hollywood stuntwoman and a movie studio wardrobe mistress, moved to the Filbert Steps in 1949 to retire. At that time the steep and rocky slope on both sides of the steps was a trash-strewn junkyard. She set about cleaning up the area and created a luxurious garden that she tended for more than 30 years. Hydrangeas, roses, fuchsias, poppies, foxglove, trumpet vines, loquat, banana, apple, plum trees; they are all there in profusion. Grace died in 1982 at ninety-six. Her ashes are buried on the hill. If you don't know the Grace Marchant Gardens get over to the Filbert Steps as quickly as you can to rejuvenate your spirit.

———•◦•———

The author with Michael McCourt
PHOTO: AUTHOR'S COLLECTION

Michael McCourt the Irish Bartender

IN AN AGE that bestows meaningless celebrity on politicos, tycoons, movie and TV personalities and social twits—a bartender with skill, wit and character like Michael McCourt is to be highly valued.

To judge Michael McCourt simply a bartender is to miss the point. He is a populist philosopher and storyteller who almost incidentally pours drinks. He is variously an impish leprechaun, or a grumpy and disgruntled warlock with an Irish choler. McCourt dispenses strong opinions on just about anything, along with strong drink—when it is required—and does so with style and self-assurance. Then, there is his near encyclopedic knowledge of his daily communicants' favorite topics: old movies, old actors, legendary drinkers, football picks, baseball batting averages and a remarkable store of other valuable, but arcane information.

McCourt can be affable, with a crooked smile creasing his Irish mug when holding an audience before supplicants reveling in his presence. But, at times he can be arch and acerbic when his patience is tried by the arrogant and the pompous. As newspaperman Bruce Bellingham, an active McCourt evangelist, says of these situations "He'll cut the bounder to the quick with his weaponry of words. Most of the time, the hapless bullies are unaware of what is happening to them. Mike delivers the punch without raising his voice."

The silver-haired Michael McCourt is from a high profile Irish family. One brother, Frank McCourt, was the author of the Pulitzer Prize-winning memoir of a miserable Irish childhood, *Angela's Ashes*, which described growing up in the Limerick slums with a neer-do-well father who spent his occasional wages and the official dole money in the nearest pub. Another brother, Malachy, has been an actor, TV talk-show host and bartender. Malachy also wrote a memoir and called it *A Monk Swimming*. The Catholic prayer called the Hail Mary includes a line "Blessed art thou amongst women..." As a youth in Ireland, Malachy heard the line "amongst women" as "a monk swimming." Logical! Alfie is the youngest of the McCourt brothers and lives in New York and has a great Irish tenor voice.

Michael McCourt was one of seven impoverished McCourt children, three of whom died in their first three years. He came to the U.S. from Ireland in 1954 when he was eighteen and after a few months joined the U.S. Air Force. As an Airman Second Class, he served as a radar maintenance technician. When he was discharged in 1958 he joined his brother Malachy, who at that time operated a saloon in New York. Michael worked there for three years as a bartender. It was his first experience behind the plank. Then, he did a few years in Southern California at Chez Jay's along the beach in Santa Monica. It was there, McCourt says, he was privileged to pour drinks for, and to drink with, pros like John "Duke" Wayne, Lee Marvin, Howard Duff and Neville Brand, who became his buddies. In 1969 he came to San Francisco and was hired as a bartender for the classic retro saloon, Perry's on Union Street. He remained there twenty-one years honing his saloon persona. He moved to Monroe's on Laguna for a while, and then to the Washington Square Bar & Grill in North Beach, Seal's Cove on the Embarcadero, the Buchanan Grill in the Marina, back to the reopened "Square," as regulars have always called the Washington Square Bar & Grill, and finally to Original Joe's in North Beach. "I was your gypsy bartender," he says now.

McCourt admits he was a hell-raiser when he was younger. "I thought I should be part of Sinatra's rat pack. I wasn't," he says now with a note of regret. Today he is a family man and lives in North Beach with his second wife, Joan. He has four children—two by his first marriage. Now adults, none are bartenders.

Many of Michael McCourt's distinguished acolytes have followed their man from one San Francisco saloon to another. These include politicians, lawyers, police officers, dockworkers, bartenders, authors, editors, reporters, musicians, advertising execs and retirees from all the above pursuits. Trading sage McCourt utterances has become a sport among them—a kind of cottage industry. Each new gem is polished and weighed carefully for its lasting truth, humor and shock value. Here are a few random McCourtisms on life, love, politics, death, taxes and other important subjects:

Saloons—"Saloons are us. Those of us left are the keepers of the flame. Saloons are drinking establishments for what is left of the drinking establishment. They are places to go to and find out who has died."

High Society—"It seems to me that those we call high society in San Francisco are just the descendants of carpetbaggers, saloonkeepers, miners and other opportunists. They were born with silver spoons in the mouths. Some of their ancestors mined that silver from the Comstock Lode. Now the hoity toity are born with cell phones in their mouths so they can call their stockbrokers."

Politics and Government—"The old politicians had a sense of humor. The new ones seem to have only a sense of their own greatness. Perhaps if they took a little glass of something each day it would improve their humor."

The Church—"When I grew up in Ireland the Church was at its zenith. We didn't dare to question anything. We were scared witless."

The 49ers—"I remember when you couldn't give away tickets to Niner's games. That was before 1981 when the Niner's won their first Super Bowl. After that we began to see the "49er Faithful" as they called themselves. They had been faithful for less than one season. Guys like Joe Montana, Jerry Rice and Ronnie Lott were really irreplaceable. Now we seem to be in the days of the forty whiners."

Death and Dying—"What a shame; people are dying these days that never died before."

Taxes—"Taxes are okay for the rich. We should really have a special tax that just benefits the disabled and the homeless."

The Mai Tai—"The other day a woman came in, sat at the bar and asked me for a Mai Tai. 'Do you see any palm trees in here?' I asked her. She settled for a shot of bourbon straight up."

Wine Experts—"I call them cork sniffers. Awhile back a guy came in and said he wanted something woody and grassy. I asked him if he wanted to start a fire or did he want a drink."

Corned Beef and Cabbage—"Some sharpie got a hold of some bad beef and sold it to the Irish. It smells like prison food to me."

They're not making bartenders like Michael McCourt anymore. He was an original. Michael McCourt died September 5, 2015.

Moose the Accidental Restaurateur

ED MOOSE, a North Beach existentialist who died in 2010, was a tireless and inspired promoter of causes—charitable, political and occasionally just plain wacky. He was also a PR genius, a do-gooder who actually did much good and, in his own words, a "ringmaster" and an "accidental restaurateur."

If he had a real life like most of us instead of the high profile, virtual reality one that flickered around him like prime time TV, he might have been a major league baseball coach, a priest (at least an archbishop), or a Democratic Mayor of San Francisco.

Whatever Edward William Moose IV was, he was also a celebrity along the lines of those he greeted and befriended at his popular restaurant and saloon the Washington Square Bar & Grill, and later Moose's—both in North Beach.

Moose wasn't just another guy with a restaurant in San Francisco. The truth is, Ed Moose had Clout—with a capital C.

One day I caught up with the big Irishman at Moose's. He removed his trademark flat cap, the type ILWU longshoreman once wore, eased his red suspenders, another trademark, and sat relaxed with a glass of wine.

Ed Moose in Washington Square Park, 2007
PHOTO: © 2015 TOM WHELAN

INTERVIEWER: Ed, without trying to put too fine an edge on it, let's deal with this existentialism business right away. You said that you were a bit of an existentialist. As we understand it, existentialists deal with what they believe to be the actuality, as opposed to the possibility. Is that the way you are?

MOOSE: Yes, I never did have long term goals. I don't plot and plan. I just go ahead and do it. I never sat down and said to myself— this is the kind of person I am going to be; this is what I am going to achieve; this is how much money I am going make. In spite of this lack of planning I have been making a living for about thirty years pretending to be a restaurateur. The Washington Square Bar & Grill was a bit of an accident. Suddenly I woke up with a saloon that served food. Then with Moose's, I didn't have a long lead time. When we sold The Square in 1990, my wife Mary Etta and I were interested in a small hotel in Sonoma. But then the old Figone Furniture Store right on Washington Square went out of business and the building became available. But I never perceived myself as a restaurateur.

INTERVIEWER: How do you think others perceive you?

MOOSE: Most people only know the public side of me, what they see here in the restaurant or what they remember of me at the Washington Square Bar & Grill. Some know me only because they have read about me in some column or other. They remember my antics, high profile events that get coverage in the newspapers and on TV. I believe most people think I am a guy who is active and likes to have a good time and likes to organize things. A ringmaster, someone who stirs things up, makes things happen.

INTERVIEWER: Do they think of you as a likeable guy?

MOOSE: Many do. Others think of me as being just the opposite. Nevertheless, I think I am outgoing and friendly with most people. I like to give people a chance and find out what makes them tick.

INTERVIEWER: What about those who think just the opposite of you?

MOOSE: There are those who haven't always agreed with what I do. There are also those with whom I don't agree, and some I simply don't like. Perhaps I am too direct and I may have offended people. If that's so, it's unfortunate and I am sorry for that. I can't draw everyone into my orbit. There are some who frequented the Washington Square Bar & Grill during its heyday, but who have gone to great lengths not to frequent Moose's.

INTERVIEWER: Why is that so?

MOOSE: Well, with some I think there was a presumption of closeness on their part that just didn't exist with me. There were others who stiffed me in one way or another. And, frankly, some were probably jealous of what they perceived as my unwarranted success. Take our softball team. It has gained enormous publicity and I simply haven't been able to put everyone in a game or take them on big road trips such as the ones we made to Moscow and Cuba. For example, there was one guy that I did take on the road, but I didn't put him in a certain game. He was furious. I told him that it was more important for me to win the game than it was for me to put him in just to make him happy. That didn't make him feel any better and that was the end of that.

INTERVIEWER: Let's talk about the softball team you coach.

MOOSE: We started a staff and customers, slow-pitch softball team in 1976. We were playing other saloons around town. It was said that to play for our team you had to be past forty, have a bad liver, or both. We had a lot of fun and we started going out on the road. In 1978 we played a pickup team in Paris from the restaurant *Le Moulin du Village* and we won. As a result Ron Fimrite wrote a long story on our team for *Sports Illustrated*. We were gaining a lot of media attention. We went to Hollywood and played a bunch of movie execs and starlets. The financier Herbert Allen, who liked to hang out in the restaurant when he was in town, owned Columbia Pictures at that time and he arranged the game. We won. Then in 1984 at the Democratic National Convention here in San Francisco, Tom Brokaw headed a team that included some heavy hitter media stars. Their team also included New York Governor Mario Cuomo. Again we won and we had so many celebrities at the Washington Square Bar & Grill during the convention that you couldn't squeeze in with a shoe horn. Brokaw asked for a rematch in New York in 1985, and we suffered our first loss on the road. In 1986 we played Boston's Fenway Park and the following day Chicago's Wrigley Field. We won both games. In 1987 Brokaw arranged for us to play in Yankee Stadium. This was big time stuff. And in 1988 we played the Foreign Correspondents' Club in Hong Kong. San Francisco Mayor Dianne Feinstein was on our team. Dianne hit a home run. Actually she dribbled a hit down the third base line but the

Hong Kong team overthrew first base. Then it became a comedy of errors and she ran the bases. We won 32 to 5 or something like that. In 1998 we were invited to Moscow where we played a Russian team that included some former Olympics athletes. I told our guys we weren't going to fly 7000 miles to lose. We won. Our last big road game was in Cuba. We played two games in Havana. We lost the first one and won the second.

INTERVIEWER: Who were some of the team members in those days?

MOOSE: There was Herb Allen, Claude Jarman, who won a special Academy Award for his part in *The Yearling*, Chris Sullivan, retired San Francisco Police inspector, Bobby Frugoli and Bobby McCambridge, who were bartenders in the restaurant, Dugald Stermer, the artist and designer, Ron Fimrite, Dave Bush, the *Chronicle* sports writer, and of course, Herb Caen, and other local business execs, media guys, bartenders, waiters and so on.

INTERVIEWER: Is that how you met Herb Caen?

MOOSE: No, Herb came to the Washington Square Bar & Grill a bit late. Tom Wolfe and Herb Gold had already written about us and we were attracting a lot of attention. *Chronicle* columnist Charles McCabe, who was a regular at that time, told me Caen will never go for you because he didn't discover you. But a little later Herb started coming in. Then he adopted the joint and wrote about us constantly. Soon he was playing first base on our team.

INTERVIEWER: Bring us up to date on the team's name *Les Lapins Sauvages*?

MOOSE: It was on our first road game, the one to Paris. A bunch of team members on the flight over were trying to come up with a name with a French flair. They decided to call the team the Wild Hares; then they translated that into *Les Lapins Sauvages*. So we became the wild rabbits since *lapin* means rabbit in French. The name stuck.

INTERVIEWER: You have a reputation of taking those softball games seriously, in fact so seriously that team members have considered you to be, well, a pain in the lower back—or even lower.

MOOSE: True. That's a well-deserved reputation. I am serious about those games. I was brought up believing that you always played to win. You always gave 100 percent. Anything less was a sell-out. That was ground into me early on. So that's the only way I know how to play. My attitude was and is: My ball, my bat, my team. I also have a theory that goes like this: Total focus on the playing field is a necessity. If you go out and play hard with total focus your chances of being injured are diminished. The dividend is winning more and having more fun.

INTERVIEWER: Let's discuss early influences. How did you get to be the Ed Moose we know today?

MOOSE: My early influences were the CHURCH, BASEBALL and the DEMOCRATS. To this day I think of them in Capital letters.

INTERVIEWER: All right, let's talk about the CHURCH.

MOOSE: I'm the product of a strong Irish Catholic upbringing. Then I went to St. Louis University run by the Jesuits where I received my bachelor's degree in philosophy and later a master's in psychiatric social work. As a kid I served as an altar boy for weddings and funerals at my parish. I got fifty cents for each. I was also an assistant grave digger and made an extra twenty five cents if I could recover the flowers before they wilted and get them back to the church so they could be used again. The church was ever-present and all-powerful in my life at that time.

INTERVIEWER: Did you have a vocation for the priesthood?

MOOSE: I thought did. I entered the seminary when I was eighteen and stayed there for about six months.

INTERVIEWER: Why did you leave?

MOOSE: Things are very complicated when you're eighteen. I just knew I should be somewhere else.

INTERVIEWER: What about baseball as an influence?

MOOSE: Of kids in those days in North St. Louis, there was only one way to distinguish yourself—on the baseball diamond. For me it was all about the spirit of the St. Louis Cardinals Gas House Gang that won the World Series in 1934 against the Detroit Tigers. Although the Gang was a bit before my time, I was old enough to know who they were and what they did. Dizzy Dean, Pepper Martin and Leo Durocher were my heroes. They were goofy and had a lot of fun but they were fierce competitors. Every game counted. In fact, every pitch counted. I'm still that way today.

INTERVIEWER: You also cited the democrats as an influence.

MOOSE: Franklin Delano Roosevelt was a god in my family. We had a photo of him in the kitchen; right along with the Sacred Heart of Jesus. If I had been forced to choose between Roosevelt and the Pope, it would have been difficult. Remember, this was during the great Depression and Roosevelt was giving us hope. Today I am greatly interested in politics, but I am also a realist. Politics are tough. When I came to San Francisco I worked first for the Catholic Archdiocese and wrote speeches for the Archbishop. The church is politics too. Later I worked for Mayor Joe Alioto as his Youth Coordinator. I was close to the powerbase and got to see how things really worked in San Francisco. I also did several years with the Urban Coalition and worked on a program that attempted reverse integration of Marin City. Later I served as West Coast Director for the Presidential Campaigns of Fred Harris and Walter Mondale.

INTERVIEWER: How did you happen to come to San Francisco?

MOOSE: I was in the army in Germany. When I was discharged I completed my master's degree and worked as a sports reporter for the *St. Louis Post-Dispatch* and later as alumni director for my alma mater, St. Louis University. Around that time I met a nice Italian girl, Mary Etta Presti, who was manager of a St. Louis cabaret. We hit it off. I also met Sam Deitsch, at that time a St. Louis saloonkeeper who was originally from New York. We hit it off too. I had a chance to cover the Rome Olympics for the *Associated Press*. When that was over I free-lanced a bit and traveled around Italy. Back in the States I decided to establish myself in that most Mediterranean of American cities, San Francisco. I moved here in 1962. Mary Etta followed and we married and moved into the first of our North Beach homes. We still live in North Beach, right across from Joe DiMaggio Playground. Then Sam Deitsch came back into my life. He too had come west and was looking around for something new. In 1973 we pooled our resources and converted an old North Beach saloon called Pistola's to the Washington Square Bar & Grill. (Deitsch died in 2002 after several years of retirement.)

INTERVIEWER: By the way how did it get its nickname, Washbag?

MOOSE: That was taxi-driver code and Herb Caen picked up on it. But those closest to the joint always called it The Square; never The Washbag.

INTERVIEWER: And the rest, as they say, is history. Ed, are you a power broker?

MOOSE: Hardly. I'm just a minor player.

INTERVIEWER: But you do have clout.

MOOSE: If you mean by clout that I know a lot of people who really are power brokers, then I suppose I have some clout. I like to think I use what clout I have for the good of the community.

INTERVIEWER: Tell us more about your friend Herb Caen. (Caen died in 1997.) Was he an influence on you?

MOOSE: Not at first, but he certainly was later. Quite simply Herb was the most powerful guy in the city. Never mind that he could make a break a restaurant, a theatrical production or whatever. When something really important was going on in the city people would call him before they called the mayor or the police chief. Herb knew everything about everything. That intrigued me. I believe he genuinely tried to use his power—his clout to use your word—for the good of the community and society in general. I try to do that. That's how he influenced me. He made it a point to know all about the people he met. He made the city much more interesting and glamorous. He made things happen. I think some of that rubbed off on me.

INTERVIEWER: Everybody knows Ed Moose—or at least claims to—but what about close friends?

MOOSE: I have a very public life and also a very private one. I know a lot of people. But real friends; true friends? There are only about a dozen or so I feel close to. There are hundreds of others who I like and admire but I wouldn't want to be in a foxhole with them. I am a totally private guy. My home is sacrosanct. I hang out there with Mary Etta. And by the way, marrying Mary Etta was the smartest thing I ever did. Without her there would have been no Washington Square Bar & Grill and no Moose's.

INTERVIEWER: The Washington Square Bar & Grill, its softball team and the Democratic National Convention in 1984 seemed to put The Square on the map. Suddenly you were a celebrity and a catalyst that made things happen.

MOOSE: Maybe a minor league celebrity, but I do believe I am a catalyst. I am a conscious catalyst. I enjoy meeting all kinds of people and putting disparate types together. That's what it's really all about for me.

INTERVIEWER: Brokaw, Jennings, Cronkite, Ben Bradlee; big media types were regulars at The Square and now at Moose's. Willie Brown is a regular. Dianne Feinstein. John York from the Forty Niners, Herb Allen. Why do they flock to your restaurant?

MOOSE: They feel comfortable in our place. We make them feel good. The place is filled with interesting people. It's all about knowing your customers. Knowing who they are and knowing all about them and then relating to them.

INTERVIEWER: While North Beach has always been unique with many appeals, you are a magnet that brings considerable economic vitality to the neighborhood. Also, we note that the St. Anthony Foundation honored you for the Annual Memorial Day Penny Pitch you founded back in 1974 to raise money for the St. Anthony Dining Room that feeds the poor. How much money has the Penny Pitch raised over the years?

MOOSE: More than a half million dollars, not counting individual pledges I have been able to acquire from various San Franciscans.

INTERVIEWER: In the beginning of this interview we called you a do-gooder who does good. Is that accurate?

MOOSE: Well, I work at it. I guess I'm just a lucky guy able to do what I like to do.

Tosca and a Whiff of Celebrity

Jeanette Etheredge and Sean Penn
PHOTO: FROM THE COLLECTION OF JEANETTE ETHEREDGE

WHEN SEAN PENN INTERCEDES to save a North Beach landmark I sit up and take notice. One assumes Penn has more pressing things to do—like going to bat for UNESCO's Haitian Relief organization, or acting in award-winning movies, which he does with regularity. But we're happy to note that saving Tosca, Jeannette Etheredge's classy North Beach saloon on Columbus Avenue, was a high priority with him.

A while back Tosca was about to go under and Jeannette Etheredge, who ran it for more than thirty years, was distraught.

There were those who spoke darkly of Tosca becoming a strip club. That fizzed for a bit, then, fizzled. Then Penn, a Tosca regular, got in touch with some buddies in New York—Ken Friedman and his chef-partner April Bloomfield—who operate the Michelin-starred Spotted Pig, a Manhattan hotspot. And faster than you can say *Shazam*, it was a done deal. Not only did Tosca continue as a beloved North Beach saloon, but when it re-opened there was a dividend—a new and improved Tosca that also served food. Under Etheredge, Tosca—its full name is Tosca Café—only served booze, ambience and attitude. Under Friedman and Bloomfield the booze, ambience and attitude continues but the pair has added Italian cuisine—what they describe as "rustic Italian fare." No reservations. Service until 1a.m. How's that for a success story?

All of this news makes me wish Sean Penn lived in North Beach. We need him. His head is screwed on straight. Imagine him saving Tosca. I wonder if he could have saved the Pagoda Palace Theater. But enough celebrity adulation. What's the rest of the Tosca back story?

Tosca dates back to November 1919 when three Italians who came to San Francisco after World War I, decided to open a bar in North Beach. They named it Tosca after the daughter of one of the founders. They opened the bar and less than two months later they received a monumental jolt—Prohibition went into effect. What to do?

One partner took off to Healdsburg to operate a brandy still. The others imported two espresso machines to steam the milk to add to the brandy. Soon, they were off and running with a house cappuccino—chocolate, steamed milk and brandy. It was a cappuccino of convenience. The hell with Prohibition.

And so Tosca has survived to this day. It made it through the Volstead Act, the Depression, World War II, the Beats, the Hippies, the Mayor Willie Brown era, and on it goes—and it still serves the house cappuccino.

Jeannette Etheredge has a fascinating family history that reads like a John Le Carre novel. Her mother Armen Baliantz was born in Manchuria. Her Armenian parents fled to Russia and later to

Armen Baliantz
PHOTO: FROM THE COLLECTION OF JEANETTE ETHEREDGE

China to escape the Armenian Genocide of 1915-1917, the Ottoman government's extermination of its Armenian minority.

Armen married import-export businessman Aram Baliantz in Tsingtao, China where Jeannette and her brother where born. During World War II the family wound up in a Japanese prison camp where they spent four years. Later they spent two years in a refugee camp in the Philippines. A woman of great conviction and courage, Armen then undertook the long journey to San Francisco and the happy sanctuary of North Beach.

The concept of sanctuary is apt when reflecting on the history of this North Beach watering hole. The near-legendary Back Room at

Tosca has been a sanctuary for Etheredge's special "friends" and harder to gain access to than the Vanity Fair Academy Awards bash. Sean Penn, of course, had an all-access pass. So did Francis Ford Coppola, Philip Kaufman, Sam Shepard, Johnny Depp, Ed Harris, Hunter S. Thompson, Norman Mailer, Bono, Nick Nolte and Nicholas Cage— just to skim some celebrity cream off the top. Nick Nolte played pool there wearing only hospital greens and granny glasses. Philip Kaufman huddled in a corner working on scripts. Bono was so taken with the North Beach landmark that he opened a bar in Dublin called Tosca.

What actually was in the famed Tosca Back Room? —A pool table and the constant whiff of celebrity. Under the new ownership we are told that the Back Room has become a storage area and perhaps a banquet room. But don't believe it. It continues to be a private haven for North Beach slumming celebrities. .

And that brings up a curious right-coast, left-coast difference. In New York, restaurants and saloons go to great lengths to display their celebrities. At joints like the much-missed Elaine's on the Upper East Side, Woody Allen and other seemingly shy folks were seated prominently in the front of the house so the rest of us could ogle them. And when I was a lad hanging out in that quintessential New York saloon Toots Shor's, one could see Ernest Hemingway at the great oval bar near the entrance. Or perhaps Jack Dempsey. Jackie Gleason was on hand to guzzle martinis by the half gallon and to display his wobbly Jackie Gleason shuffle.

But here in San Francisco we pretend to hide our A-list celebs like cloistered Trappist monks who murmur only to themselves and to a higher authority. In the case of Tosca the higher authority was (and I assume still is) Jeannette Etheredge.

But how did Jeannette Etheridge acquire so much juice with our culture icons—pop and otherwise? She can thank her mother for that. Shortly after Armen Baliantz arrived in San Francisco she opened her own restaurant at Sansome and Jackson using an emerald ring for bank loan collateral. Later it moved to Pacific and Battery. She called it Bali's and soon it was the in-spot for a diverse group of dancers, writers and filmmakers, and of course their hangers-on and wannabes. Armen, a beautiful and scintillating woman, was a ballet enthusiast and she loved to cosset the stars. She befriended Rudolf Nureyev when he defected from the Soviet Union in 1961. And she became a close friend and confidant of Mikhail Baryshnikov. Everyone who was anyone—as they once gushed in the society columns—turned up at "Madam Bali's" She was beloved. She held court with caviar, champagne and Russian vodka. Her rack of lamb, marinated in pomegranate juice made *Godfather* genius Coppola—an Armen Baliantz acolyte—almost weep with joy.

Daughter Jeannette grew up in this regal milieu. She got to know the cast of characters in her mother's life. Then in 1980 Armen convinced Jeannette to buy Tosca. She said it was the first bar she entered when she came to the United States and she grew to love it. For several years Armen and her Bali's restaurant shared the North Beach spotlight with Jeannette's Tosca saloon. Bali's closed in 1985. Armen Baliantz died in 2007.

Soon Tosca with its coveted Back Room became hallowed ground. And it looks as though it will continue to be just that. Thank you Sean Penn.

Francis Ford Copolla, 2011
PHOTO: DREW ALTIZER / NORTH BEACH CITIZENS

Citizen Francis Ford Coppola, Winemaker

HOLLYWOOD BIGWIGS MAY CONSIDER San Francisco a small, jerkwater outpost in a beautiful geographic setting, but nevertheless we have had a surprising number (more than our share really) of film actors, producers and directors of towering stature. Sean Penn, Robin Williams, Saul Zaentz, Phillip Kaufman, George Lucas and Francis Ford Coppola come to mind.

Their star power burnishes our city. But perhaps the brightest of these luminaries is Coppola, multi-Academy Award winner and creator of the iconic *Godfather Trilogy* and the devastating look at the Vietnam debacle, *Apocalypse Now*. Coppola hangs out in North Beach.

These days our attention is not on Coppola, the godfather of the *Godfather*, but rather on Coppola as a concerned and involved North Beach neighbor who continually strives to make our home turf as good as it can be and better than it is at this point.

Coppola founded an organization called the North Beach Citizens. He gathered a group of local merchants and residents to discuss how they could address the issue of homelessness in their neighborhood. At that meeting he said "My idea is that if the City is made up of many, many neighborhoods, any neighborhood that wanted to do something positive would have to at least know who they're doing it for. So part of this has to be a linking of the North Beach people who are homeless to the North Beach community."

It wasn't really a complicated idea. Coppola articulated the concept that is the North Beach Citizens' mission statement—Treat each individual homeless citizen as an individual, rather than as a generic public annoyance. And then do something about each on an individual basis.

Since Coppola founded the group in 2000 the North Beach Citizens has gotten More than 200 persons off the streets and into permanent homes. And, it has been reported that the City of San Francisco spends $61,000 per year on each homeless individual using public services. Coppola's group spends $18,000. It's funded almost entirely by individual contributions.

I wanted to talk to Coppola about this but, unable to pin him down to an eyeball-to-eyeball meeting (the timing was awkward), we exchanged question and answer e-mails with him. Now, we know that e-mail is a curious and sometimes maddening medium in which to work. It can be both cursory and thoughtful at the same time. This e-mail exchange shows Coppola's great interest in most of the issues I raised, but he was also a bit elusive. He chose not to respond to a couple of questions. So be it.

INTERVIEWER: Can you tell us about this organization you founded, the North Beach Citizens? How did this come about?

COPPOLA: It was an idea that formed when I realized that more and more homeless people were gravitating to North Beach. There was more and more panhandling. I felt that homelessness could be dealt with in the community on a community basis, especially if we could look at these people as citizens—as part of the community.

INTERVIEWER: I have the sense that North Beach Citizens does much good work but has quite a low profile. Is this your intent?

COPPOLA: We tend to focus closely on the work we are doing on behalf of the North Beach community and for the clients we are serving in this community. We try to use imaginative ideas to help redeem people who seem to have lost their way. We're entirely self-financed by the people of North Beach. And that's out of necessity since government or city funds are too elusive.

INTERVIEWER: Since you obviously travel a great deal how involved are you personally with the North Beach Citizens organization?

COPPOLA: I believe in the formula that charitable organizations tend to need to become somewhat self-supporting in about seven years. This demonstrates that the idea was right in the first place and that there is a need for the work to be done. So, at first I was essential to the development and the funding of the North Beach Citizens. Now, with the emergence of a strong board of directors and a capable staff and administration I am less involved. However, I still do try to participate.

INTERVIEWER: I know you are an active and busy person. You seem like you have a lot on your plate. For example, I note you are involved in revitalizing the historic Napa Valley, Inglenook Estate vineyards and winery. Can you tell us something about that move and what your plans are?

COPPOLA: We have been blessed, I would say, to be able to restore the historic Inglenook winery which was founded in 1879. And in this recent step we've acquired the trademark and name once again.

INTERVIEWER: I also see that your plan for the Inglenook Estate calls for the famed winemaker Philippe Bascaules to become the Inglenook Estate manager and winemaker. Can you tell us a little about that decision and your thinking behind it?

COPPOLA: There are many elements involved in creating a world-class premium wine estate. First, to make great wine. Second, to have made great wine fifty years ago, or one hundred years before that. Third, to have a management and winemaking team that has been associated with and made great wine at their previous situation. Fourth, to be located in the epicenter of a great wine region and in the specific site considered best in this region. For example, the Medoc in Bordeaux and Rutherford in the Napa Valley. Fifth, to enjoy a great heritage and history. Sixth, to have the original property intact, and with as much of it in pristine condition. Seventh, to have sufficient acreage of vineyards to make enough wine that it may be enjoyed throughout the world. Most Bordeaux First Growth properties have a similar number of hectares. Inglenook is the same. And finally, to be owned by a private family. Preferably a family who lives on the property.

*

As I stated, communicating with someone by e-mail can be both cursory and thoughtful. Coppola obviously was thoughtful in his responses to my questions about the North Beach Citizens, his founding of the organization and his continuing involvement in it. But it was with real passion that he addressed my questions about his Napa Valley wine estate. That was not only thoughtful; it was instructive, educational, if you will.

I did ask him two more questions by this imperfect e-mail system. I took a shot at seeing if he would tell me anything about his future film projects. And then, as a last, pitch, I invited him to comment on any subject he chose. Below, as you will see, I struck out.

INTERVIEWER: As I said above, you seem an extremely busy man—pulling yourself in several directions at once. May I ask you this final question? Any plans for film in the future? Anything you would care to reveal?

COPPOLA: (No reply.)

INTERVIEWER: Anything else—about any subject—you would like to add?

COPPOLA: (No reply.)

I can live with that. I tried to sneak one in and it didn't work. As I said, he is a busy man. And busy people need to be guarded in how they marshal their energy. That's one of the principal reasons they are successful. And no matter how you measure success, Francis Ford Coppola is brilliant and successful.

And the North Beach Citizens and his California winery are two of his finest legacies.

Claude Jarman Jr. and The Yearling

Claude Jarman Jr.
PHOTO: COURTESY CLAUDE JARMAN JR.

I LOVE GOING TO THE MOVIES in real movie houses and I'm going to tell you about a film I saw many years ago with a youngster named Claude Jarman Jr. in a starring role. The movie, which came out in 1946, was called *The Yearling*. It was based on Marjorie Kinnan Rawlings' Pulitzer Prize-winning story about a backwoods kid named Jody who adopts a fawn and bumps up against the realities in the life of an impoverished family struggling to succeed. Ultimately it becomes necessary for Jody to shoot the fawn. Gregory Peck played Jody's father, Jane Wyman, his mother.

I loved the movie and I admired Jarman. Prior to *The Yearling* I had never heard of him. MGM Studios conducted a nationwide talent search for an unknown kid to play the part of Jody. Jarman, the son of a railroad accountant, was ten years old, in the fifth grade and living in Nashville, Tennessee. His only acting experience had been in school plays. The studio sent him to Hollywood for a screen test and he got the part. The boy got terrific reviews and won a Special Juvenile Academy Award for his performance. It was presented by Shirley Temple. With that success under the boy's belt the Jarman family moved to Southern California to be where the Hollywood action was and for almost a decade Claude Jarman Jr. was in ten more movies.

Back then several other kids received the Juvenile Oscars. Shirley Temple was the first in 1935 and Claude got his in 1947. Others were Deanna Durbin, Mickey Rooney, Judy Garland, Margaret O'Brien and Hayley Mills who got the last one in 1960. At that point the Motion Picture Academy did away with kids' Oscars and from then on gave out the big ones regardless of the actor's age. Retroactively, in 1983, they gave Claude Jarman the big one.

Recently, San Franciscan Jarman—now a tall, blue-eyed, senior citizen with a full mop of silver-gray hair, and lean and rangy in the Gary Cooper mold—reflected on those Hollywood years as an MGM contract player: "I was lucky. It was the Golden Age of MGM. It was the best studio in Hollywood and I was part of it."

Asked what he thought of his success at the time, Jarman said. "I had nothing to compare it to. I thought 'Doesn't everyone have this?' I had my own dressing room, my own makeup person, my own wardrobe person. I went to school in a two-room school house on the MGM lot in Culver City.

"There were about twelve kids under contact to MGM. Elizabeth Taylor, Jane Powell, Margaret O'Brien and Dean Stockwell among others," he recalls.

Adult stars were frequently matched romantically by MGM to gain press excitement. Occasionally, the studio arranged publicity photo dates for its kid actors and it arranged several such photo dates for Jarman, thirteen at the time, with child star Margaret O'Brien, then ten. "Hardly Richard Burton-Elizabeth Taylor stuff," Jarman says.

Following his success in *The Yearling* Jarman appeared with some of Hollywood's biggest stars and moved from playing a ten-year-old kid, to a teenager, and then to a young adult.

After playing in a few movies like *High Barbaree* with Van Johnson and June Allyson in 1947, and *The Sun Comes Up* with Jeanette MacDonald, Lloyd Nolan and Lassie in 1949, Jarman was picked for a young adult role in the big John Ford movie—*Rio Grande*—starring John Wayne, who played a cavalry officer.

"That was my favorite film to work in. It was filmed on location in Moab, Utah and I got to ride horses which I loved. Most of my contact with John Wayne was actually filming various scenes. I played a young trooper who was John Wayne's son," Jarman remembers.

Another career high point was a 1952 film called *Hangman's Knot* that starred Lee Marvin. "I was seventeen at the time. Marvin was a larger-than-life tough guy. He befriended me and I rode around Hollywood with him in his red Thunderbird convertible. I took in everything he said and did."

There were a few other films like *Fair Wind to Jamaica* and *The Great Locomotive Chase*, but that was about the end of Jarman's Hollywood career. He was growing up and very few youngsters make the transition to major adult roles.

Jarman and his parents moved back to Nashville in 1950 where the young man finished high school, entered Vanderbilt University and studied pre-law. He graduated in 1956. Then, having been in the university's military OCS program (Officer Candidate School), he joined the Navy, became a Lieutenant JG and served three years.

"Because I was colorblind I was assigned to the PR staff of the commandant of the Seattle naval base. Then after a couple of years I was sent to Hollywood, this time not as an actor, but as a member of the Armed Forces PR office where I worked with studios making movies about the Navy," he recalls.

"My wife was from Birmingham, Alabama so when I was discharged in 1959 we moved there and I got a job working for a Birmingham advertising agency.

"I was doing some work for the John Hancock Insurance Company, which decided to open an office in San Francisco. They offered me a job in that new office and I accepted. I had never been to San Francisco," Jarman said.

Almost immediately he met Glenn Dorenbush, a charismatic tippler, bar philosopher and publicist. Dorenbush, always quotable, had an inside track with San Francisco columnists like Herb Caen and Charles McCabe, so top saloons like Perry's and the Washington Square Bar & Grill employed him to get their names in the papers. Jarman was quotable himself and had that magic Hollywood background. Overnight he became part of San Francisco's well-lubricated saloon culture. Although not much of a drinker, he enjoyed, and still enjoys the sociability of bars and counts several bartenders among his friends.

Soon Jarman became involved with the San Francisco International Film Festival, founded in 1952 and one of the oldest events of its kind in the country. He was named to a film selection committee that included Shirley Temple Black, writer and nightclub owner Barnaby Conrad and novelist Herb Gold. Jarman and Temple were on opposite sides of a controversy that arose over the notorious Swedish film *Night Games*. The board voted whether or not to show the film. It had overtones of sexual perversity, lesbianism and incest—then considered highly controversial film material. Jarman voted to show it. Shirley Temple voted against it and denounced the film as "pornography for profit." It developed that while the other board members had watched the film to consider it for the festival, she had not seen it. The film was shown and the world did not end.

Later that year Jarman was named Executive Director of the influential event.

In 1974 Mayor Joseph Alioto tapped Jarman as Director of the city's Cultural Affairs Department which meant he oversaw operations of the opera house and other civic arts organizations—as well as the film festival.

He took another shot at acting and appeared in an episode of the TV production "Centennial." He also served as Executive Producer of the well-regarded "rockumentary" on Bill Graham and the Fillmore Auditorium. And to bring you up to date on that earlier lucky and magical period in the life of Claude Jarman Jr., he appeared as a special guest as a past Oscar winner at both the 1998 and 2003 Academy Awards ceremonies.

Always a dedicated social saloonist, he hung out at the Washington Square Bar & Grill and played short stop for proprietor Ed Moose's quirky softball team, *Les Lapins Sauvages*. He was once again enjoying the limelight. Then in 1980 the well-placed and popular young San Franciscan was recruited by the Shaklee Corporation where for five years he ran its public relations and travel departments. Then in 1986 he founded his own travel agency and operated it until recently when he finally shut it down.

These days Jarman is sitting back and smelling the roses of a successful career that took him from Hollywood actor to San Francisco public figure. Most weekdays he can be found hanging out in North Beach, perhaps having lunch with buddies at Original Joe's. He is a contented man. His Academy Award Oscars sit on the mantelpiece in his home. He has fathered seven children, including two daughters with his present wife Katherine who he is helping with her real estate ventures.

Asked the inevitable question—"What if?" he concludes: "If I had not been picked out of my school for that movie role in *The Yearling*, I would probably still be in Nashville instead of San Francisco."

Saul Zaentz the Oscar Machine

THE BARE BONES OUTLINE for the life story of Saul Zaentz could be a plot for one of the many movies he made during his lifetime. And therein lies a story waiting to be told.

Young man from a Russian-Polish, Jewish immigrant family in Passaic, New Jersey with a passion for jazz, baseball and movies, drops out of high school and supports himself by gambling. In 1942 he joins the army to see the world. He sees it and in four years attains the rank of sergeant major and gets his first view of the city by the Golden Gate. Still footloose when he is discharged in 1946, he goes to St. Louis, largely because he is a fierce St. Louis Cardinals fan. There, between home games, he attends business college for a couple of years, then picks up and drives west—all the way to San Francisco.

An employment bureau sends him to a phonograph record distributing company. He gets the job. He does everything—fills orders, packs records, talks to disk jockeys. He learns the music business. Soon Saul Zaentz meets jazz impresario Norman Granz who lures him back east. While working for Granz, he goes on the road managing concert tours with Duke Ellington, Dave Brubeck, Gerry Mulligan and Stan Getz.

Then in 1955 Zaentz returns to San Francisco and joins Fantasy Records. By 1967, with the help of a few investors, he purchases the company.

What Saul Zaentz purchases is a company with a diverse group of artists including Dave Brubeck, Vince Guaraldi and Cal Tjader—even X-rated comic Lenny Bruce. Plus a bunch of unknown "new thing" rock groups. One day, to find out what he has in the archives, he listens to a local rock group from El Cerrito called the Golliwogs that has been playing in pass-the-hat joints. The sound—a kind of "swamp rock"

Saul Zaentz in Tunisia during the filming of "the English Patient," 1995
PHOTO: FROM THE COLLECTION OF THE SAUL ZAENTZ COMPANY

we would identify it today—appeals to him. He calls the Golliwogs into his office—one of them, John Fogerty, is a Fantasy warehouseman. Zaentz suggests that if the group changes its name, Fantasy will give it a recording contract. Fogerty and his bandmates change the name to Creedence Clearwater Revival.

In 1968 Saul Zaentz and Ralph J. Gleason, iconoclastic music and pop culture columnist for the *San Francisco Chronicle*, get together and Gleason becomes a VP for Fantasy. Soon, the two are dreaming and scheming. They decide to make a movie. Zaentz has always wanted to do that. He wants to make *One Flew over the Cuckoo's Nest*, the Ken Kesey novel. But the rights are owned by actor Kirk Douglas who wants to play the part of the quirky Randle Patrick McMurphy. Negotiations slide and Saul passes. He and Gleason are hell-bent to make a movie. They do. It is called *Payday*. The late San Francisco Bay Area novelist Don Carpenter writes the screenplay and actor Rip Torn plays the lead in this gritty music biz drama of an amoral country-western singer.

Pauline Kael, film critic for *The New Yorker*, praises the movie. In February 1973 she writes: "Financed by Fantasy Records and completed last year, it was brought in for fewer than seven hundred and eighty thousand dollars. Universal, Warner Brothers, Twentieth Century Fox and Columbia all turned it down for distribution—though it is doubtful if they could bring in a film that looked this professional for three times that amount." "Hmm," thinks first-time filmmaker Saul Zaentz when he reads Kael's *New Yorker* review.

One day in 1974 he gets a call from Michael Douglas, Kirk's son, who later becomes a close friend. Michael Douglas has acquired the rights to *One Flew over the Cuckoo's Nest* from his father who apparently no longer wants to play McMurphy. "Still interested?" Michael Douglas wants to know. Absolutely! And in 1975 Zaentz's first major movie effort, *One Flew over the Cuckoo's Nest*, directed by Czech émigré Milos Forman and starring Jack Nicholson as McMurphy, sweeps the top five Academy Awards including Best Picture.

In just more than twenty years and seven films later, Saul Zaentz-produced motion pictures are awarded twenty-two Oscars—three for Best Picture. After *Cuckoo's Nest*, Zaentz makes *Three Warriors* in 1977 and *Lord of the Rings* in 1978. Then in 1984, in his second collaboration with Milos Forman, comes *Amadeus*—eight Oscars including Best Picture and Best Director. He follows this with *Mosquito Coast* from the Paul Theroux novel. It stars Harrison Ford. Then in 1988 comes *The Unbearable Lightness of Being* from the Milan Kundera novel. It is directed by San Francisco's Philip Kaufman. It is honored with three Academy Awards nominations. In 1991 Zaentz brings out *At Play in the Fields of the Lord*, a powerful drama about man and his primitive nature.

Then, in 1996 Zaentz produces *The English Patient* from a novel by Michael Ondaatje. It sweeps nine Academy Awards including Best Picture and Best director with those honors going to Saul Zaentz and Anthony Minghella, son of an Italian immigrant to Britain. At the Academy Awards Ceremony in Hollywood Saul Zaentz also receives the prestigious Irving G. Thalberg Memorial Award "For a consistently High Quality of Motion Picture Production." *The New York Times* says "He invests in his own films, possibly a singular distinction, and helps bring them to life with a hands-on style. He is perhaps the last of the great independent producers."

His final film was *Goya's Ghost* in 2006, a Milos Forman collaboration starring Javier Bardem and Natalie Portman. Although it received some good reviews it was not a successful venture.

If you're keeping track, Saul Zaentz films have garnered twenty-two Oscars. How does that measure up with other San Francisco movie heroes? Francis Ford Coppola has fourteen including the Irving Thalberg Lifetime Achievement Award. George Lucas has one—the Thalberg Award. Who has the most Oscars for Best Picture? It's a tie between Sam Spiegel (*On the Waterfront, Bridge over the River Kwai,* and *Lawrence of Arabia*) and Saul Zaentz (*One Flew over the Cuckoo's Nest, Amadeus* and *The English Patient*).

Not bad for a kid from Passaic, New Jersey.

At this point in our Saul Zaentz screenplay we must fade from a head shot of a smiling, white-bearded Santa Claus in a double-breasted tuxedo on stage at the 1996 Academy of Motion Picture Arts and Sciences Oscar presentations, to an impish, man in a large sunny office in Berkeley where this writer interviewed him several years ago.

INTERVIEWER: Music, especially jazz, seems to have been your highest priority following your acquisition of Fantasy records. Was there a defining moment when you began seeing yourself as a filmmaker?

ZAENTZ: I had been interested in films and filmmaking for a long time. I always loved movies and the theater. By the time Gleason joined me at Fantasy I knew I wanted to make films. Ralph was a good catalyst and sounding board for me. Right from the start we knocked around ideas for making a movie.

INTERVIEWER: When you made *Payday* and it received some good reviews did you think it was going to be a one-time thing or did you begin thinking of yourself as a filmmaker?

ZAENTZ: Well, I didn't begin thinking of myself only as a filmmaker. I was interested in a lot of things—not just making movies. In fact, I love jazz and still love the record business. Sure, the idea of making more films was appealing, especially since Ralph and I proved to ourselves that we could make one.

INTERVIEWER: Why did you never set up shop in Hollywood?

ZAENTZ: Because I love San Francisco—especially North Beach. That's why I came west in the first place. San Francisco is a big, small town. There's a lot of freedom here, a lot of intellectual curiosity and artistic ferment. There always has been. San Francisco has a long history as a music center. Jazz was always important here. Look at the rock movement and the vitality it has given the area. Fantasy recorded Allen Ginsberg reading *Howl* and also Lawrence Ferlinghetti who was the focal point for the Beat movement here. Do you know there was a burgeoning movie industry here way back in the early days of films? Chaplin made films here, for example. It just isn't necessary to live in Southern California to make motion pictures. I don't dislike Los Angeles. It's just that I like San Francesco much more. I am a San Franciscan although I came from New Jersey.

INTERVIEWER: Who are some of your favorite motion picture directors?

ZAENTZ: Well, obviously Milos Forman since he directed some of my most successful films. But there are others. Woody Allen comes to mind. Sydney Lumet, Stanley Donen, and Akira Kurosawa. Those are a few right off the top of my head.

INTERVIEWER: How about actors?

ZAENTZ: Spencer Tracy. He made it all look so easy. Or Marcello Mastroianni. Do you remember Federico Fellini's movie *La Dolce Vita*? Mastroianni steps right into the water in Rome's Trevi Fountain and walks through it to give a flower to Anita Ekberg. Beautiful scene.

INTERVIEWER: By all accounts your career continues to go up and up and shows no signs of topping out. You must be very proud of what you've accomplished so far.

ZAENTZ: Let's put it this way. There's a wonderful Yiddish word *naches* that denotes the best attributes, the best connotations, of the word "pride." I remember once Sonny Rollins, the great jazz tenor saxophonist, said that he recorded twenty-five years for Fantasy and never had a written contract. Now that is something. There was trust on both sides and both sides can take pride and pleasure in that—*naches*. So in that sense, I can be proud of some of the things that have brought me pleasure in my life.

INTERVIEWER: Does it get any easier?

ZAENTZ: No! It's a lot of fun, but it doesn't get any easier.

INTERVIEWER: Saul, I know you were born on February 28, 1921. Do you ever think of retiring?

ZAENTZ: When Kurosawa was in his eighties he said "I'm not only thinking of my next film, but I'm thinking of the one after that." I met Kurosawa. I was at a small dinner party with him once and we talked about the subject of retiring. He said to me "People like you and me should die on the movie set." I was honored that he included me in that sentence.

INTERVIEWER: What if you and I made a movie of your life story? Would it be big at the box office?

ZAENTZ: It would bomb. My story doesn't have enough drama."

•

Saul Zaentz died in 2014 at ninety-two.

Kevin Brown and Live Worms

KEVIN BROWN, an artist of considerable stature whose paintings sell for lively prices in his North Beach gallery Live Worms, has been a San Francisco resident for more than forty years. Kevin, his wife Marianne and their black Lab, Scout, live in a Cow Hollow three-story, frame and shingle dwelling he calls their "little house on the hill."

And in that "little house on the hill" are scores of Kevin's paintings done since he retired as an international airline pilot—yes, that's right— and decided to re-create himself as an artist, find a studio and apply brush to canvas.

How did this happen?

On a typical overcast July day in 2003, Kevin Brown was strolling along in North Beach and noticed a "For Rent" sign at 1345 Grant Avenue. It was the site of an old neighborhood landmark, Figoni Hardware, which had occupied the premises since the early 1900s but had gone out of business. Kevin had grown tired of his artists' material cluttering up the Cow Hollow premises and needed a place to paint and display his impressionistic and abstract oils and acrylics—bold canvases with a lot of built-in tension.

"I found the owner and took a look at the place. It was perfect, a large deep space with a very high ceiling," he recalls. He made a deal on the spot and a few days later brought his stuff over from the house and moved in. While rummaging around and cleaning the place he found a small black slate blackboard. On it in chalk were the words "Live Worms." Remember the days when hardware stores sold live bait?

"What a great name for my gallery," he thought at the time.

So the former international airline pilot—he retired in 1996 after more than thirty years as a 747 Captain with Pan Am and Delta—put the Live Worms blackboard in the window and hung some of his own

Kevin Brown, Live Worms
PHOTO: IRIS ROWLEE

paintings on the walls. They were wildly leaping abstracts with heavy strokes and squiggles and splashes of intense color. Almost immediately he began selling his work, which at that point he called "old fashioned modernism."

Now, more than ten years later, Live Worms is a popular hangout on Upper Grant Avenue and Kevin is a well-recognized North Beach character in a neighborhood overflowing with loopy artistic types. Not only is this modest and mild-mannered artist showing and selling his own work for $500 to $5,000 or more, but he makes his gallery space available to other artists and charges them a small fee—$150 per day during weekdays, $250 per day on weekends and $750 for Friday, Saturday and Sunday. If they sell any of their work, and they almost always do, Kevin doesn't dip into their pockets for a commission— almost unheard of in the high-powered art world.

Soon Live Worms began attracting artists who came not only from North Beach but from all around Northern California. Suddenly there was an art scene on Upper Grant Avenue where once the Beats had gathered to drink red wine, recite poetry to jazz backgrounds and to celebrate their benevolent but urgent lifestyles. Today the old neighborhood is renewing itself and once again becoming a center for artistic expression. Other galleries, live music and unusual shops are cropping up and attracting a lot of foot traffic. To suggest that Live Worms is providing a high dose of cultural nutrients to a reviving North Beach is not an overstatement.

Now a youthful seventy-five, Kevin has been exercising his creative juices with paint and brushes since he was a kid—with time out in the cockpit of a 747 of course. His father was a U.S. Navy officer and the family moved around a lot. When young Kevin attended Arizona State University on a scholarship he majored in Art but, not believing he could make a living as an artist, he also took pilot training and then spent five years in the U.S. Air Force. Well, one thing led to another and that led to Pan Am and Delta.

Yes, we all know retired airline pilots are not particularly known for being eccentric free spirits who open art galleries and have smudges of paint on their pants. But Kevin made that unlikely transition. He executed a 180-degree power turn from using the left side of his brain to using the right side. Mathematicians and airline pilots use the left side and artists and dreamers, the right side. Everybody knows that, right?

So this eccentric and brainy left-side-right-side guy has led a somewhat skewed life. Some of his friends refer to him as the Gertrude Stein of North Beach. If that's a reach for you, try this: Kevin, the Cow Hollow guy, has become an important benefactor of artistic expression in the old North Beach neighborhood just as Stein was in Paris. He operates an art gallery called Live Worms on Upper Grant Avenue. Stein operated a salon in 1920s Paris. Now if we could only bring back Allen Ginsberg to give a reading of *Howl* at Live Worms.

———•———

Ron Spinali King of the Italian Sausage

Ron Spinali, the Italian sausage butcher
PHOTO: AUTHOR'S COLLECTION

LET'S TALK ABOUT a North Beach Italian butcher shop and social club for the food obsessed and a butcher who's an expert on Italian sausage.

San Francisco's North Beach–to paraphrase Hemingway–is a moveable feast. Yes, the neighborhood is changing, evolving might be a better word, and that's good. But some things don't change, in fact they just get better with age, and that's good too. Take Little City Market, the Italian butcher shop at the corner of Stockton and Vallejo Streets.

In the old days, in the 1940s, there were more than a half dozen Italian butcher shops in North Beach. Today, Little City is the only one in the neighborhood and one of the few old-fashioned, independent butcher shops in the city. The others dropped out along the way. Higher rents, labor costs, dwindling profit margins, all took their toll. The rise of the ubiquitous supermarkets with their self-service, shrink-wrapped meats, poultry and fish—and their shrink-wrapped prices—made the independent butcher shops seem superfluous. Many of the old Italian butchers retired and their offspring preferred other career paths.

But Little City Market, like the little engine that could, just keeps rolling along. Why? What's the secret to its longevity?

The answer, according to Ron is to be more than a butcher shop and much more than a butcher.

Little City is an informal neighborhood clubhouse—a social center if you will—for those who like to chat about food and its preparation. It just happens to sell top quality meats—select beef (corn-fed for steaks), pork, "rose" and "white" veal, chicken and eggs from nearby Petaluma, and other products like Little City's hand-made Sicilian and Calabrese sausages from old family recipes.

"Many of our customers have educated palates and are interested in good food as part of the good life. They not only come from the neighborhood but from all over the Bay Area. Some drop in only once a month to stock up on special cuts of beef, pork and veal," says Ron.

It's not uncommon for customers to drop by for a few sausages for example, and remain for an hour discussing spices, herbs, cooking techniques and sharing recipes. There's even a comfortable bench for those inclined.

Little City dates back to 1941 when Ron Spinali's father George opened in North Beach. The Spinali family is from Sicily. Patriarch, Luciano Spinali came to San Francisco at the turn of the century and joined a long line of Sicilian immigrants who became fishermen. He operated his own fishing boat at Fisherman's Wharf. His son, George Spinali became—as Ron tells it today—"a meat cutter." He worked for Buon Gusto, a long-gone Italian market in North Beach. A generous but frugal man, George Spinali saved his money and opened Little City Market—meat, produce and dry products like pasta, rice and beans—at 570 Green Street. It remained there until 1951 when he moved to the present site at 1400 Stockton Street.

When George Spinali died in 1972, Little City Meats went to Ron who had begun working for his father when he was eight. Then, in turn,

Ron brought his son Michael into the operation when he was sixteen. Mike became a skilled journeyman butcher and later succeeded his father as owner. "I work for my son now and that's as it should be," says Ron. Until her death a few years ago, Ron's mother Angelina kept the books from a tiny cubbyhole above the shop. She was also the genius behind "Nana's Pasta Sauce," a big seller at Little City.

Ron Spinali is friendly and personable and has a broad knowledge of cuisine, especially Italian, and is eager to share it with customers. Not only does he provide uncannily accurate cooking times for the roasts, braises and sautéed dishes he suggests, but he maintains a file of personally-created recipes to help nervous cooks climb the hurdle of doubt about their abilities. Little City is the kind of place where you might intend to drop in for a pound of hamburger but after considerable discussion, leave with some beautiful veal shanks and the Little City recipe for osso buco.

Along with the select meat products, Little City features a wide variety of other items to enrich the lives of their customers. None is more important than the house *demi-glace*, the intense veal bone stock, reduced to its essence over hours of simmering, that Ron produces on the premises. "A little demi," he says "adds a richness and body to almost any dish."

But perhaps the most sought out products at Little City are the unique Italian sausages. Most are pork-based, but it also offers lamb sausages and has developed special festive sausages for each major holiday. Some are hot with the addition of fiery red or green peppers. Little City's Christmas sausages, Sicilian in style, are redolent with garlic and a touch of provolone, the distinctive Italian cheese. It's Italian sausage with an attitude.

As stated earlier, the once predominantly Italian neighborhood of North Beach is evolving. It's becoming more multi-cultural as Chinese and other ethnic groups overlap—not without occasional stresses and strains. However, the balanced view on the future of North Beach—shared by Ron—is that an international city like San Francisco is enriched and strengthened by various ethnic cultures.

Mary Risley (right) and student
PHOTO: COURTESY MARY RISLEY

Tante Marie Wanted to be a Flower Child

MARY RISLEY WANTED TO BE A FLOWER CHILD but Julia Child's cookbook changed her mind. Readers may be excused if they don't recognize the name Mary Risley but her pseudonym Tante Marie may ring a bell.

Before I learned that Mary Risley was Tante Marie of the famed Tante Marie Cooking School in North Beach, I almost invited her up to my house for dinner when she gave me a handful of fresh rosemary from her Telegraph Hill garden.

That was a few years ago when I ran into her weeding her cliff-hanging vegetable plot up on Chestnut Street. I watched her for a while, and then struck up a conversation. I had just come from the shop of my buddy, butcher Ron Spinali down the hill. Mary asked what I had in my market sack. I told her I had been shopping and picked up a fine leg of spring lamb I planned to roast that evening for the family dinner. That's when she plucked the rosemary and handed it to me saying lamb and rosemary went together like—well, liver and onions, one of Mary's comfort foods.

I thanked her and fortunately asked her name. When she told me, I put lamb and rosemary together—I was talking to the highly-regarded cooking school teacher known as Tante Marie. Mary Risley took the name Tante Marie from a famous French cookbook author; much like some French woman might consider naming a cooking school after the American Fanny Farmer.

Mary no longer tends that unique vegetable garden on Telegraph Hill city government land. It's been replaced by your plain old, garden variety garden. A nearby resident objected to the Tante Marie garden—maybe she just didn't like vegetables as a kid—and Mary, at that point in the midst of writing a cookbook, gave it up.

When she started the Tante Marie Cooking School back in 1979 Mary Risley was a hands-on, in-your-face cooking teacher. Now, more than thirty years later the school is still going strong but Tante Marie no longer teaches there on a regular basis. Instead she devotes herself "to traveling, eating and writing which always was my lifetime goal," she says. These days she has a jam-packed website—Tante Marie's Newsletter—in which she writes about food, cooking, travel and whatever else comes to mind, including a recipe of the month.

Mary's interest in food and cooking stems from her childhood in New England. "When I was about nine I was already making brownies, fudge and chocolate cake from my *Baker's Chocolate Cookbook*. I collected recipes and was a good organizer," She says.

Mary Risley did not go to college. Instead she went to secretarial school in Boston and took a low pay job in the investment business. In 1968 she got wanderlust. A friend told her she had an "Out West Personality" and she drove cross country to San Francisco with everything she owned.

"I wanted to be flower child but by the time I got to San Francisco it was too late to start putting flowers in my hair, so I worked as a temporary secretary for several years. All I knew was that I didn't want to work in an office for the rest of my life. I wanted to be a consultant; that sounded like a good thing.

"Then the wanderlust returned and I took off. I studied cooking in London at Le Cordon Bleu and later in Paris at the famed La Varenne cooking school," she recalls.

Today she credits Julia Child with setting her off on a career. Back in San Francisco in 1973 she moved into a flat on Leavenworth Street and handed out flyers offering evening cooking classes in her kitchen. "That first time eleven students came to my flat and I taught them everything I learned from Julia Child's *Mastering the Art of French Cooking*. The night before a class I would read a chapter of Julia's book and then use what I learned the next evening," she told me.

In 1979 she moved into the present space on Francisco Street and the Tante Marie Cooking School was born. Today it is a thriving business and Mary Risley has achieved considerable renown in the hot, high-profile world of food and cooking.

She's also noted for her work with Food Runners, the San Francisco non-profit organization she founded in 1987 that redistributes food leftovers to the hungry. Her work with Food Runners gained her a singular honor in 1998 when the influential James Beard Foundation gave her its Humanitarian of the Year Award.

If cooks wore military-style uniforms instead of those nerdy white jackets, Mary Risley's chest would be full of medals. Awhile back the San Francisco Professional Food Society presented her with its Lifetime Achievement Award. In 2008 she was presented with Channel Five's Jefferson Award. And in 2005 she was honored by the North Beach Citizens and received their Community Recognition Award.

Earlier, in 1997 *Bon Appetit Magazine* honored her as Cooking Teacher of the Year and in 1998 the *San Francisco Chronicle/Examiner* named her one of the ten most influential people in the Bay Area.

Oh yes. Did I ever invite Mary Risley up for roast lamb? I'm still thinking about it.

———•◦•———

Randall Kline
and the Transcendent Moment

Randall Kline
PHOTO: JAY BLAKESBERG / SF JAZZ

SFJAZZ, San Francisco's highly-acclaimed, year-round music festival, is one of the most imaginative and creatively programmed performing arts events anywhere. Audiences embrace it with enthusiasm and it enjoys an international reputation. So what makes it so good?

Certainly it's the music—adventurous and stretching the limits of what we usually consider jazz by delving into musical roads frequently less traveled.

The creative thrust behind SFJazz is Randall Kline, Executive Artistic Director, who founded the event in 1983. At that time he hoped for the best and kept his fingers crossed. Today he recalls that the best he could hope for then was that his fledgling, money-losing concerts called "Jazz in the City"—which began with a few modest, small scale performances—would make it to its second year and then perhaps go on from there.

As Randall Kline tells it, he got lucky. The event received a few small local grants and then scored with a grant from the National

Endowment for the Arts which had just set up a jazz program that proclaimed jazz a national treasure. Jazz was being considered right up there with established European arts forms. Randall and his Jazz in the City were in the right place at the right time and flourished.

Luck plays some role in almost every endeavor, but Kline gave luck a better than even chance by being a highly imaginative and creative guy with good management skills. He built SFJazz; he manages it and controls the programming. He runs it.

During an interview I called him the creative force behind his brain child. He backed off just as a good CEO should. He sounded like an NFL coach crediting everyone from the players to the fans for success. But, the fact is Randall Kline is the decision maker for SFJazz. He's the coach. And he stands at the intersection where the luck stops and creative vision begins.

It's difficult to get the engaging but modest Randall Kline to acknowledge that he is a creative guy. Although, checking out what he's accomplished in the last thirty years puts him right up there with imaginative movers and shakers in San Francisco. Trying to hang the creative laurel wreath on Kline's brow is difficult as fathoming a free form jazz solo. He prefers to refer to himself as a conduit, an aggregator and an organizer who receives artistic programming input from various sources. And it's true. Randall Kline is a good listener. His ears are open to music of all types that come to him through visits to concert halls, music clubs, through his car radio and his iPod. He is also keen to hear what musicians and others tell him.

What then was the road that led him to where he is today—leader of an internationally-acclaimed, year-round performing arts event in a city that takes its cultural offerings very seriously?

"I grew up in a Massachusetts household that treasured music. My mother loved Broadway and movie show tunes and cast albums. She also appreciated symphony and opera. My father was more jazz oriented. He was a good amateur piano player. So I grew up listening to all kinds of music including the major jazz artists. I also listened to a lot of pop and I was into the so-called British invasion—the Beatles, the Rolling Stones and the Animals," he told me.

But his real jazz epiphany occurred when he dropped out of college back east and on a whim moved to the Bay Area in 1975. He had applied to the Berklee School of Music in Boston and was accepted. His instrument was the stand-up bass. While he was preparing for Berklee he took a required class in ear training at College of Marin.

"I discovered that the school had a great jazz tradition. There were teachers there who had studied with Stravinsky, Schoenberg and Milhaud who had worked in that idiom," he said.

Instead of returning to the East Coast and entering Berklee, he entered San Francisco State University in 1982 as a performance major. In his senior year he produced a few jazz concerts to make some school money. "I proceeded to lose every dollar I had so I dropped out of college for the second time and got a job at a San Francisco nightclub called the Boarding House. One thing led to another and here I am," he said. And that was the path to enlightenment for Randall Kline.

To get a better and more accurate sense of the man I believe it's instructional to shift here to a Q and A format—undiluted Randall Kline.

INTERVIEWER: This baby of yours is called SFJazz. But your programming goes far beyond jazz. What are your personal programming guidelines?

KLINE: Jazz is at the center of what we do. And over the years we have booked almost every major jazz artist. It's true that I have programmed a lot of music that's not really jazz. But true jazz has always been inspirational. It has influenced and been influenced by other musical forms and persuasions. So I am always on the lookout for musical connections. I want to dot the lines from one music to another. Although, for example, it's quite easy to see the connections between African drumming and jazz, some connections between musical forms are not so easily seen. But that doesn't mean they don't exist.

INTERVIEWER: Give us a couple of examples.

KLINE: Well, in 2011 we programmed Randy Newman who you wouldn't really characterize as a jazz artist. He's known more for his pop songs with twists of irony and satire. He wasn't presenting jazz in the true sense but our crowd loved him. We also booked Rosanne Cash—hardly jazz. She's carrying on the American country musical tradition of her father Johnny Cash. So the word "jazz" has more than a narrow definition. People have become highly eclectic in their musical tastes. They have a great curiosity.

INTERVIEWER: So what have you done to feed that curiosity?

KLINE: I've tried to establish an aesthetic that accommodates many musical tastes.

INTERVIEWER: And that aesthetic that accommodates many musical tastes is your taste. Right?

KLINE: I suppose so. I just love great music.

INTERVIEWER: How do you define great music?

KLINE: I like to define it as music that provides me with an over-the-top experience—music that can take me somewhere. I'm a sucker for that kind of experience. I want to be moved. I want that isolated transcendent moment that makes me soar.

INTERVIEWER: Give us a few examples of musical transcendent moments you have experienced—not necessarily on performances of SFJazz?

KLINE: I'll give you three examples, although I have many. Everyone does. My first example is Mariza, the Portuguese fado artist. My transcendent moment with her took place a while back in the Anspacher Theater (part of New York City's Public Theater group). I don't speak or understand Portuguese so I didn't know what she was conveying in words but I knew the spirit of what she was conveying by a group of factors that made this a transcendent moment for me. It was a combination of her craft, her artistry, the place in which she was singing and the audience. It all came together for me that one night. My second example is Joe Lovano, the great tenor saxophonist. For a long time I have known that Joe Lovano was a fine jazz artist, but I confess his music didn't get to me on a visceral level. Then all of sudden, one night at the Bitter End nightclub in New York City—suddenly I got it. He played in a trio format—George Mraz was the bassist and Al Foster was on drums. I was standing in the back of this small crowded club. They were at the top of their game. It was transcendent. Then there was a night at the Lyceum Theatre in Brooklyn. Kayhan Kalhor the Kurdish artist played his *kamancheh,* an ancient Persian stringed instrument. He was accompanied by a string quartet called Brooklyn Rider. The sheer beauty of Kalhor sketching those exotic melodies on that classic instrument just blew me away. Again, it was a transcendent moment for me.

Yes, Randall Kline is an aggregator, a conduit and an organizer. But his creative genius is his desire—his need really—to direct others to the musical creativity he has discovered in those transcendent moments.

Tony Serra is Greedy for Life

Tony Serra
PHOTO: ERNEST BEYL

FOR ITS SIZE you might think that feisty San Francisco has had more than its share of eccentric, over-the-top lawyers. Silver-tongued, sometimes gun-toting, principled or unprincipled defenders of raw justice or bookish, law book, bookworms — have all paraded through the legal history of the city. A few who come to mind are Vincent Hallinan, Charles Garry, J. Martin McGuiness, Melvin Belli, Jake Erlich, Al Bendich and Paul Halvonik—all courtroom brawlers for the downtrodden, for the disenfranchised, for the impoverished and the marginalized. But of all these legal drum beaters, there's one who marches at the head of this parade.

He's J. Tony Serra, perhaps the fiercest of these courtroom fighters—and perhaps also the most dedicated and most effective of them all. He's the guy you want to defend you in the U.S. legal system if you have a staggering uphill fight, impossible or preposterous charges against you, and maybe face the rest of your life behind bars. Yes that would be Tony Serra—a true legal maverick, law textbook radical, a battler, skilled in maneuvering in the arcane, sometimes draconian world of the American justice system.

But don't take my word for it: Here's what some of his peers have to say about the man:

"Not since Clarence Darrow has a trial lawyer attracted such envious attention in court. Not since Byron has there been a more poetic, passionate defender of liberty."—San Francisco attorney John Keker.

On Tony Serra's book *Walking the Circle: Prison Chronicles*: "Slam bam, yabby, yabby warden. Tony Serra busts out a beauty here and made a true believer out of me. Knock on wood."—San Francisco activist Wavy Gravy.

"A life filled with passion, trouble and general shit-kicking may be the best life to have, but probably only if you're Tony Serra, wily defense lawyer, generous supporter of perilous causes, devoted custodian of just about everyone except himself."—San Francisco author Herbert Gold.

The bare bones of the Tony Serra story are these:

A native San Franciscan, Tony excelled in high school and went to Stanford University where he was a letterman athlete. He majored in philosophy with a specialty in epistemology—no less. He recalls: "When I graduated there was nowhere out there in the real world with jobs for those who had studied epistemology. I was from the so-called upper, lower class. My father worked and put food on the table. My family wanted all the good things in life—jobs and material manifestations of success. But for some reason, this was absent in me and has been all of my life.

"But I was filled with what we might call romantic fallacies. So I took on the image of an Ernest Hemingway—an expat who wanted to explore, experience life and write about the experience. So, logically to me at that point, I took off for Tangier to write poetry. I sat around in the cafes writing in my journal. I became part of the scene. I dabbled in raw opium, kif and hashish.

"Then I realized that I wasn't going to be a poet, at least not a good one. I had misguided myself with the romantic fallacy. So I came back to San Francisco and went to law school at the University of California in Berkeley where I became heavily involved in the free speech movement.

"But then I experienced another romantic fallacy. I decided I would become a mafia lawyer. But I was disabused of that idea by the Haight-Ashbury and the Summer of Love. It was exhilarating to be a hippie. There was free love and everyone was naked and that was exciting."

Tony passed the bar and began to practice law. He gravitated to unpopular causes and went on to become one of the most famous defense lawyers of our time—a demon for social change through litigation.

But Tony Serra adopted a curious lifestyle. It was the lifestyle of most of his clients. "Early on, in an LSD session, I took a vow of poverty. I pledged never to capitalize on the practice of law. I denounced capitalism, private ownership of property and major business. I rejected probate law that allows one generation to pass accumulated wealth to another generation.

"Today I own nothing but old clothes and artifacts. I have no real property, no money in the bank, no stocks, no trusts. I live from hand to mouth." Tony's clothes are secondhand and comfortable. He drives old beat-up cars that fall apart on him. Aren't lawyers supposed to get rich, wear bespoke suits and drive Porsches? That's not Tony.

Tony Serra operates out of what he terms Pier Five Law Offices—not on the San Francisco Embarcadero's Pier Five anymore, but now in a large open space in North Beach above Enrico's on Broadway. It was once occupied by Finnochio's, the city's long-gone female impersonator night club. Most law offices echo the severity and gravitas of the courtroom. Tony's law office echoes a 1960s Haight-Ashbury party pad. The psychedelic décor reflects Tony's interests. There's Middle Eastern and American Indian art on the walls along with prison drawings and paintings from death row inmates.

So lawyer Tony Serra has become a celebrity in our celebrity-ridden culture. Books are written about him. He also writes his own books. There was a movie in 1989 about a Chinatown murder case in which he won an acquittal for the defendant. "But it was butchered," he says.

There are those observers of this celebrity culture who would refer to Tony Serra as kooky or loopy. But they are only marginally correct. If you had called Tony Serra kooky or loopy in the old days you probably would have gotten into a fist fight with him. These days—he's 80 now —he might just give you a lashing with his sharp tongue. On the other hand he might just use the occasion as a jumping off point to nail you on a point of legal logic.

Over the years Tony Serra has defended a wide range of individuals, causes and direct action groups—some of which have resorted to violence—that jolt the minds of those in our lock-step society. Black Panther leader Huey Newton, the White Panthers, the Hells Angels, Earth First, the New World Liberation Front, the Symbionese Liberation Army, Brownie Mary and other champions of marijuana for recreational or medicinal purposes.

Twice he has served prison terms in California's Lompoc Federal Prison Camp for his strong stance against paying taxes that he says go to support America's wars. His method of resistance? He does not file tax returns. And failure to file has landed him in the slammer. He accepted his incarceration in good spirit and wound up advising inmates on their problems.

And while Tony Serra has been defending lost causes he has won numerous awards from influential law groups and received accolades from his legal peers.

Recently I asked Tony how long he planned to keep on truckin' in the courtroom. He's been at it for fifty years with an uncanny degree of success. Tony responded: "Well, we all have different wicks in our candle, so I can't really say. But I don't abuse myself. I'm not an alcoholic. But I acknowledge that occasionally I get zonked smoking a mild weed for relaxation. I smoke for sacramental purposes." He continued: "I want to continue in the courtroom while I am of sound mind. I'm greedy. I'm greedy for life. But when the time comes, I want to die in the courtroom while having a heart attack as I'm making my final arguments in a case—and my client will be acquitted."

————•·•————

Acknowlegements

AFTER WRITING THIS BOOK I considered attempting to create a formal and exhaustive bibliography. It sounded like a good idea at first. Later the concept seemed so daunting I scrapped it in favor of these acknowledgements for the following reasons: First, I have been working on this book on and off for a number of years and my sources of information varied from the books I read and the people I talked to during those years—hundreds of books and hundreds of people. Second, for a long time I didn't even know I was writing a book. I was writing a series of short essays, some of which appeared in somewhat altered states in a number of publications. Third, it occurred to me that if I gathered these essays in some order I might have a book and happily my publisher Grizzly Peak Press agreed. And finally, the point is I didn't formally keep track of sources. Hence the idea of a bibliography eluded me. This isn't to say that I don't recall where I got ideas for my essays. In most cases I recall quite clearly and I'm going to acknowledge those sources now.

Much of my research was acquired eyeball-to-eyeball, ear-to-ear with denizens of San Francisco, especially the North Beach neighborhood. Here are some of them:

Enrico Banducci—Looming large in these acknowledgements is my friend Enrico, the impresario, restaurateur and storyteller. It was Banducci who over glasses of wine and plates of spaghetti and countless cups of coffee at his Enrico's Coffeehouse, led me through the North Beach labyrinth of clubs like his hungry i, with comedians, folk singers, other entertainers and local characters.

Michael McCourt—Bartenders are a great source of information and Michael McCourt, the quintessential Irish bartender has been a great source.

Ed Moose—My friend Ed Moose was not only a great restaurateur, he was a great storyteller. And I got a lot of them from him.

Stanton Delaplane—Delaplane, the great *San Francisco Chronicle* columnist, encouraged me to use just the right verbs in the elusive pursuit of exemplary prose. He once told me this about writing: "It's something like barbecuing a steak. It's not the time on the fire. It's all those turns in the marinade, the loving touches with the fork and brush."

Lawrence Ferlinghetti—Lawrence figures large in my life. In truth, I idolize him. Salty, acerbic, always spot-on in his judgments, he gives me a lot of his precious time and I appreciate it. Lunch with Lawrence Ferlinghetti is a profound experience.

Herbert Gold—Herb is both an early and a late bloomer. He published his first novel when he was a youngster in Paris and many more since then. As I write this, sixty years later he's publishing another novel. Herb is one of my heroes—a writer's writer, and always finds time to talk to me about my stuff.

There were many books that served as sources of inspiration and information to me. Among these were:

Americans and the California Dream: 1850-1915 by historian Kevin Starr, (Peregrine Smith, Inc. 1981)

The Madams of San Francisco by Curt Gentry, (Signet Publishing Company 1965)

Broadway North Beach – The Golden Years by Dick Boyd, (Cape Foundation Publications 2006)

Good Life in Hard Times by Jerry Flamm, (Chronicle Books 1978)

The Parade's Gone By by Kevin Brownlow, (University of California Press 1968)

Imperial San Francisco: Urban Power, Earthly Ruin by Gray Brechin, (University of California Press 1999)

The Portable Beat Reader edited by Ann Charters, (Penguin Books 1992)

How to Talk Dirty and Influence People by Lenny Bruce, (Playboy Press 1963)

Of great importance to me in the writing of this book has been City Lights Booksellers and Publishers, the iconic gathering spot in San Francisco's North Beach. This was, and still is, a hangout spot for me, a place to read the Beats and about the Beats—in fact a place to read about almost anything.

I must also single out my family for inspiration and help with this book. My wife **Joan Beyl** has always been my best editor. I rely on her to keep me accurate, logical and focused. My daughter **Laurel Beyl** has been a loyal reader and has impeccable judgment in what to put in and what to leave out. And my son **Jeff Beyl**, a published writer himself, has been a sensitive sounding board. He's into geology and can make rocks come alive and speak on the page.

There are other individuals to acknowledge as well:

Merla Zellerbach—Merla was once my editor at the *Nob Hill Gazette*. I recall her fondly. One day she said "How would you like to write a history of San Francisco bordellos?" My response was "Do I get an expense account?" I didn't, but my appetite for the story was whetted and I did a three part series.

Susan Dyer Reynolds—Susan, Editor-in-Chief of the *Marina Times*, is wonderful to write for. Open to anything that crosses my mind.

Earl Adkins—Earl is publisher of the *Marina Times*, another open mind, easy to work with. He praises my work and that's always nice.

Lynette Majer—Lynette was my editor at *Northside San Francisco* and now at the *Marina Times*. She's a careful, no-nonsense editor who knows how to nourish a writer.

When I first conceived this book I thought of it as a series of written profiles or anecdotes that would stand alone and be informative and entertaining. But when Daniel David, Publisher of Grizzly Peak Press, and Donald Ellis, Executive Editor, agreed to publish it, they believed the book would be enhanced if it included images—etchings, drawings, line cuts, photographs. And, of course they were right. That was when I turned to my gal pal and graphic designer **Sara Brownell** and asked for her help. I knew Sara from the days when she served as Production Manager/Graphic Designer for the *San Francisco Bay Guardian* and later

Art Director for *Northside Publications.* Sara jumped in and became the curator of the images you see in this book. She did such a good job that the publisher decided to have her design the book. She has been an invaluable contributor to this project.

And for the many other friends not mentioned here who have been sources for this book, I gratefully acknowledge their contributions.

ERNEST BEYL
San Francisco, March 2015

About the Author

ERNEST BEYL is a San Francisco writer who has long been fascinated by the history of his city and the characters, then and now, who have made it buzz with excitement. He writes not only about San Francisco history, but also about food, restaurants, jazz, fly fishing and whatever else strikes his fancy. His monthly column for San Francisco's *Marina Times* gave him the idea for this book of Sketches from a North Beach Journal.

As a kid he was fascinated by the writer Richard Halliburton, a romantic loner who spent his life on what he called *The Royal Road to Romance*—title of his first book. Wishing to travel that royal road himself Beyl joined the marines at eighteen which seemed the most practical way to see the world. Following peacetime service in Asia and the Pacific he attended Stanford University and that set him up for a career in journalism. He became a reporter for the *San Francisco Chronicle* and the *San Mateo Times* and later a freelancer for magazines and newspapers. He did a stint as a Hollywood press agent which led him to Sun Valley, the Idaho ski resort, where he served as publicity manager and where he met an early idol, Ernest Hemingway.

These days he spends his time on his newspaper column, reinventing himself as a playwright (a new discipline for him), and playing the Chinese gong for the Green Street Mortuary Marching Band (an activity he got into while researching a magazine story). He's married, has two sons and a daughter and lives on San Francisco's Telegraph Hill.

Index